THE GUINNESS BOOK OF
FLAT RACING

THE GUINNESS BOOK OF
FLAT RACING

GUINNESS PUBLISHING

CONTENTS

Published by Guinness Publishing Ltd
33 London Road, Enfield, Middlesex EN2 6DJ

Editor: Simon Duncan
Designer: Neil Randon

© Guinness Publishing Ltd, Gerry Cranham
and Christopher Poole and Associates 1990

'Guinness' is a registered trademark of
Guinness Superlatives Ltd.

Typeset by Ace Filmsetting Ltd, Frome,
Somerset
Printed in Italy by New Interlitho SpA, Milan

British Library Cataloguing in Publication Data
Cranham, Gerry
    The Guinness book of Flat racing.
    1. Great Britain. Flat racing
    I. Title   II. Poole, Christopher
    7984'3'0941
ISBN 0-85112-344-9

PREFACE

When Gerry Cranham first approached me to write the text for the *Guinness Book of Flat Racing* I was delighted to accept. Cranham's standing as a photographer of the equine scene is paramount as anyone fortunate enough to have copies of the *Guinness Guide to Steeplechasing* or the *Guinness Book of Steeplechasing*, both written by Richard Pitman, will know. This companion volume has been many months in production in line with Cranham's insistence on the highest standards being maintained.

Gerry Cranham's library of racing pictures must be among the most extensive in the world and together we have chosen more than 300 colour and black and white photographs to illustrate this celebration of Flat racing. Gerry and his sons, Mark and Paul, have also taken many specific shots to accompany the text, an operation which has involved them in countless hours of work and thousands of miles of travel.

Although an old-established sport, racing is part of today's entertainment business. It is a substantial leisure industry from which more than 100,000 people earn their living directly or indirectly when studs, sales companies, the on- and off-course betting industries, marketing and catering and so on are taken into consideration. But, essentially, horseracing is about fun and a sense of occasion. Few people are unaffected by the sheer physical beauty of a racehorse in action. Few can shrug their shoulders in indifference at the excitement generated by a high-quality race in which jockeys and their mounts strain every muscle in a battle for transitory glory.

Gerry Cranham, perhaps as no other photographer, can capture that supreme moment with magnificent clarity and insight. *The Guinness Book of Flat Racing* is, first and foremost, a publication of outstanding pictures. I am thrilled to be associated with it and feel sure that you will be delighted to look at it time and time again.

Christopher Poole

ACKNOWLEDGEMENTS

Many people have assisted with the compilation and production of this book and Gerry Cranham and Christopher Poole would like to acknowledge the help of them all. However, some names are worthy of special mention. George Ennor, chief racing reporter of the *Racing Post*, and Graham Rock, a regular contributor to *The Times*, gave most valuable advice on the text; Valerie Burholt undertook much painstaking research and provided all the statistical information contained in these pages in addition to assisting with the production of the final draft; and Gerry's wife, Nan, kept the whole show on the road, particularly during the selection, identification, indexing and captioning of hundreds of photographs, a most exacting task demanding constant supplies of coffee. Mark and Paul Cranham took additional photographs and Mark's assistance with the selection and captioning process is also gratefully acknowledged.

Simon Duncan, our Editor at Guinness Books, and Neil Randon, the Art Director, proved of the greatest help and encouragement. To these people and everyone else who contributed in so many ways, our most grateful thanks.

FROM SMALL
BEGINNINGS...

The evolution of the modern-day Thoroughbred racehorse has taken about 60 million years from the prehistoric Eohippus, standing just 15in (37.5cm) high and exclusive to the North American landmass, to the sleek and refined descendant now endemic to virtually every part of the globe except the Arctic and Antarctic polar regions. The early horse went undomesticated until perhaps 3000BC. At least this is the period in which the first records were kept of horse trading. Before that man hunted the horse for food but our own primitive forebears soon realized that its potential as a beast of burden was as important as using the animal for the cooking pot.

Credit is normally given to the people of north-east Asia for being the first equestrians. However, other sources suggest the Chinese and the Brahmins of India. Evidence is scanty but by the Third Millennium BC several of the Asian civilizations were horse-power based and some kind of informal and impromptu racing was probably taking place on a wide spectrum. Horses were among the speediest creatures from earliest times. Never equipped by nature with horns, sharp teeth or possessing an aggressive demeanour, their ability to run fast was their sole defence against predators. This ability was, quite literally, harnessed by early man for use in commerce, war and sport. But many

centuries passed before the formalization of horse racing as we know it today and it was the English, with their committee mentality, who first drew up rules and regulations for the proper conduct and discipline of a sporting pastime which, by the reign of King James I was sweeping the civilized world.

Considering how structured horseracing is today it is curious that the Jockey Club, the hub around which the sport in England has revolved for more than two hundred years, is so poorly documented. In fact, the origins of this august and powerful body are obscure. All that can be stated with any certainty is that the Club gradually evolved from gatherings of aristocrats and gentlemen who met at the Star and Garter in Pall

Previous page: The ancient Roodee, Chester's charming city-centre racecourse where the city walls provide a fine vantage point for non-paying spectators.

Below: The Jockey Club's imposing headquarters in Newmarket. To the far left, next to the white building, is the entrance to the National Horseracing Museum.

Right: The Jockey Club Stewards, pictured at the Club's administrative headquarters at Portman Square in 1984. The then Senior Steward, Lord Manton, is seated flanked by (left to right) Louis Freedman, the Marquis of Hartington, who became Senior Steward in 1989, Miles Gosling, Sir Cecil 'Monkey' Blacker and Sir John Astor.

Mall. These sportsmen and gamblers would collect to discuss racing, coursing, hawking and cock fighting and to settle wagers. Certainly the Club existed in a well-defined state by 1752 when we find a first printed reference in the *Sporting Calendar*. An auctioneer named John Pound, with premises in Covent Garden and at Newmarket, announced in that publication, 'a Contribution Free Plate is to be run for at Newmarket on Wednesday, April 1, by horses the property of Noblemen and Gentlemen belonging to the Jockey Club at the Star and Garter in Pall Mall'. By 1771 the Jockey Club had leased a coffee house in Newmarket and was in the process of acquiring other land and freehold property in the little Suffolk market town to which the racing fraternity was attracted by the huge expanse of surrounding heathland, ideal for hunting, racing and other country pursuits.

The private members' Club which was to rule the Turf without hindrance until the formation by statute in 1961 of the Horserace Betting Levy Board to gather, control and redistribute finance from gambling turnover, was comparatively late on the scene at Newmarket. That part of the East Anglian Fenlands has a more ancient association with the horse. Queen Boadicea (Boudicca) was quartered at the nearby village of Exning and trained her celebrated charioteers on Newmarket Heath before the sacking of Colchester and St Albans. King Charles I followed his father, James I, in using the Heath as his playground and with the Restoration and the crowning of Charles II Newmarket became, in all but name, the capital of England with the Merry Monarch conducting much of the business of state from his hunting lodge just off Newmarket High Street. It was to this establishment that Charles II brought his mistresses including Nell Gwyn, the handsome Louise de Querouaille and Frances Teresa Stewart, 'La Belle Stewart', the model for Britannia. During those heady days and nights given over to the pleasures of sport and the bedchamber, racing became the vogue of England's ruling classes with the King himself, known as Old Rowley after the name of his favourite hack, acting the role of arbiter for any disputes arising from the races.

This was to be the self-appointed task of the Jockey Club in later times. But for some years,

although interest in racing was spreading rapidly throughout the Kingdom, the Club's regulations held no sway outside Newmarket and it was not until the mid-19th century that its jurisdiction became recognized beyond racing's headquarters. That the Club achieved such standing was, in large part, due to the eminence of three members, Sir Charles Bunbury, Lord George Bentinck and Admiral Rous who, between them, succeeded in streamlining and enforcing the Rule Book and waging war on Turf malpractice which had been widespread.

Bunbury established the prestige of the Jockey Club; Bentinck's great gifts as an admin-

Previous page: Sir Winston Churchill looks down from the wall of the Jockey Club Committee Room.

The austere Jockey Club Stewards' Room at Newmarket (right) with its celebrated horseshoe table. When alleged miscreants appeared before the Stewards they stood facing the all-powerful rulers of the Turf, giving rise to the expression 'being on the carpet.'

istrator continued its evolution, while Rous brought integrity and reform to the sport in addition to framing the handicapping system and weight-for-age scales that are largely unaltered to this day. Each in his own way was a dictator and Rous, in particular, was frequently self-opinionated and dogmatic, being entirely convinced that his view was always correct. But it is unlikely that the sophisticated, well-ordered sport of racing that we know today would have been possible without the vision and dedication of this trio of early pioneers on whose work a great sporting industry now rests.

The very name 'Jockey Club' contains a double paradox. No active professional race rider has ever been admitted to membership—Sir Gordon Richards was made an honorary member on his retirement—nor is the body a club in the usual meaning of the word. The first contradiction can be explained by a change in usage of language. Two hundred years ago the word 'jockey' was defined as meaning 'one who manages or has to do with horses'.

Although the Club may originally have held some social and recreational aspects, not unlike the celebrated gentlemen's clubs of St James's, London, it developed along specialist and quite different lines since from inception its member-

ship was made up entirely of 'sportsmen'. From early times, the executive powers of the Jockey Club have been vested in Stewards. Since about 1770 three such senior officials began to be elected by the membership on a three-year basis. The Senior Steward, in effect a chairman, always carried a high profile and such dominant figures as Bunbury and Rous held that office for far longer terms by the simple device of offering themselves for continuous re-election in the sure knowledge that they would be unopposed. These days there are normally six Stewards but the role of Senior Steward remains highly influential and virtually no proposed alteration in the Rules of Racing or any reform is likely to succeed without his approval.

The Jockey Club retains a position as one of the pillars of the sporting establishment although the absolute power of this self-perpetuating oligarchy is open to challenge in Common Law. A Royal Charter of 1970 reinforced the Club's power which, in practical terms, would only be diminished by Act of Parliament. However, over the past two decades the Jockey Club has made considerable strides towards presenting a more democratic and acceptable image. In 1977 women were first accepted as members, and a Public Relations Manager now holds briefings for members of the racing Press. But it remains elitist, conducts its meetings in secret and still replenishes its ranks by private invitation to a narrow, upper-class section of society. Should an industry such as professional racing and breeding which, with bookmaking and other peripheral occupations provides employment to more than 100,000 people, be left in the hands of amateurs? The Jockey Club, fully aware of public opinion, has recently appointed a salaried Chief Executive, Christopher Haines, to work in harness with the present Senior Steward, Lord Hartington. But an underlying level of disquiet seems likely to remain until such time as the Club significantly broadens its membership base. (Readers will find a fuller discussion of what the Jockey Club actually does in a later chapter, 'How Racing Works'.)

The need for a central administration to organize, control and discipline racing is not disputed but in those days which preceded fast and comfortable travel from one part of the country to another, racing was organized on a strictly local basis. When all but the wealthy had to walk from their homes to the racecourses and the horses themselves were ridden from stable to track, regional, let alone national, racing was inconceivable. So the conduct of fixtures usually rested in the hands of local worthies such as mayors and officers of trading guilds, often with the assistance of the militia and the gentry. Typi-

cal of such early race meetings was that run on Shrove Tuesday in 1540 at the Roodee in Chester. The mayor, one Henry Gee, was instrumental in arranging the event and donated a silver bell. Apparently, his efforts were well supported by the City Guilds and the fixture was a great success. Chester's almost circular racecourse remains essentially unchanged to the present day and has a reasonable—if unprovable—claim to be England's oldest-established track.

Folklore, if not documented history, suggests the Roodee—flat ground near the city centre on the banks of the River Dee—has been in more or less continuous use for racing since the time of the Roman charioteers when, you will recall, Boadicea was sharpening her hubcaps on Newmarket Heath. By the reign of Henry VIII the Roodee was also in use for foot racing and a dangerous and unruly game known as foote-ball, played with a leather sphere presented by the Drapers' Guild. The object was to carry or kick the ball from a cross on the Roodee to the house of either the mayor or the sheriff but so many injuries were caused in the resulting free-for-all that foote-ball, at least in Chester, was outlawed

soon afterwards. How long the ban lasted is unrecorded but Sealand Road, the present home of Chester City FC, is located within a few hundred yards of the racecourse to which soccer can claim an historic link from the Tudor period.

Hawking, tennis and a predilection to the ladies held King Henry's attention more than racing but his daughter, Elizabeth I, is reputed to have ridden more than ten miles to attend a fixture at Salisbury when in her seventieth year. Nor was that her only visit to the historic and beautiful Wiltshire course. She was there with her favourite, the handsome young Lord Essex and other courtiers shortly before Drake sailed from Plymouth to rout the Spanish Armada. To mark the occasion a special race for a golden bell was organized. The trophy is said to have been worth £50, a huge sum at the time, and was won

by a horse owned by Lord Cumberland, one of the leading breeders of his day.

Salisbury's greatest claim to fame is the Bibury Club, founded in 1681, and acknowledged to be the oldest racecourse members' club in existence anywhere in the world. Although racing on the attractive Salisbury course with its spectacular views across the city dominated by that magnificent cathedral spire has never been of the highest class, the track has an important role in the sport's history. In 1766, for example, the outstanding horse Gimcrack first raced there, returning two years later to win the Silver Bowl. The following season an even more celebrated racehorse, the unbeaten and peerless Eclipse, carried off the same prize. Starting at 10–1 on, he scored unchallenged, as usual. Salisbury's ability to attract the occasional top-flight star has continued through to modern times and it was on this course that the 1971 Derby and Prix de l'Arc de Triomphe hero Mill Reef made his debut.

Yorkshire has always been a hotbed of racing and in Doncaster and York boasts two of England's foremost courses. The Darley Arabian

The cupola which surmounts the clocktower of the Jockey Club (left) to give a distinctive feature to the Newmarket skyline.

The Morning Room (below) with the famous portrait of Eclipse over the fireplace.

stood near York and founded one of racing's greatest breeding dynasties. His son Flying Childers, after whom a race at Doncaster is run to this day, and Eclipse's sire Marske were other notable racehorses and stallions to emanate from that part of the country. Doncaster's Town Moor course, the setting for the St Leger, the world's oldest Classic race, has been in use since 1595—the track is shown on townplans of that date. The Knavesmire was once York's place of public executions and was where the notorious highwayman Dick Turpin met his end. It has been used as a racecourse since 1731 but records show that as long ago as 1530 there was a meeting in the nearby Forest of Galtres and another on Acomb Moor.

The small town of Pontefract, situated between Doncaster and York, also holds an honoured place in the history of racing. Although the course there is of relatively minor importance these days it was a setting for important fixtures in Stuart times. The vast and impregnable fortress of Pontefract Castle was then looked upon as holding the key to domination of the North. Built on the orders of William the Conqueror by the Norman knight Ilbert de Lacy, its

Captain the Hon. Nicholas Beaumont (above), Ascot's much-respected Clerk of the Course, poses at his desk, the walls covered with the names of Ascot Gold Cup winners spanning nearly two centuries.

Above right: The elegant simplicity of the Jockey Club at Newmarket showing the tiled entrance hall.

The Jockey Club gallery (right) with its unique collection of engravings and photographs of Club members dating from the early 1800s. By kind permission of the Jockey Club

walls were so massive that it withstood three sieges during the Civil War. During the last of these in March 1648, with a Roundhead army camped around the fortress, a race meeting was held within sight of the castle.

During the Civil War racing also became a feature on the Downs at Epsom, a racecourse now synonymous with the Derby, the world's most celebrated and imitated horserace. Around the world there are now more than forty races with the word 'Derby' as part of their titles but the Derby at Epsom remains the most famous event on the international Turf calendar. Dubbed by Disraeli the 'Blue Riband of the Turf', the great race was inaugurated in 1780 by Edward Stan-

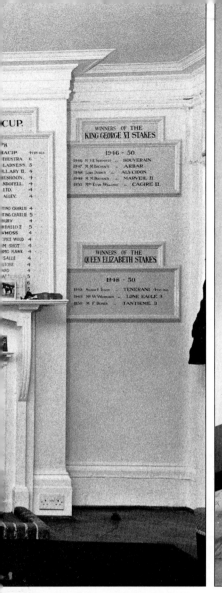

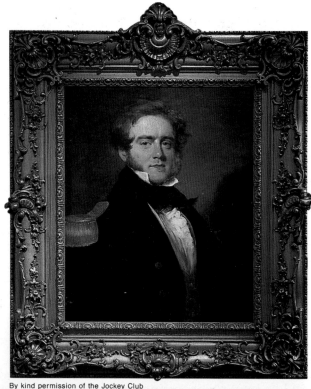

ley, 12th Earl of Derby who had also been instrumental in starting the Oaks the previous year. The Earl was, apparently, a pleasant man who liked nothing better than to show his hospitality by entertaining friends at his country house near Epsom which was named The Oaks. He enjoyed racing but his true sporting passion was for cock fighting and he angered his wife, the actress Ellen Farren, by staging that questionable pastime in the drawing room after dinner!

For all its global fame now, the Derby was initially looked upon as quite an ordinary event but gradually began to attract huge crowds of racegoers from London, just fifteen miles distant, and Doncaster's St Leger was obliged to concede the status of premier Classic to the Epsom race. The Derby, at one time run over a mile, now forms the centrepiece of England's five Classic events and, at 12 furlongs, like the Oaks, forms a natural distance progression between the 1,000 and 2,000 Guineas—both at 8 furlongs—and the St Leger which takes place over a mile-and-threequarters. Both the 1,000 Guineas and Oaks are limited to three-year-old fillies but three-year-olds of either sex are permitted to take part in the other three Classics although in modern times it is unusual to see fillies race in either the 2,000 Guineas or the Derby. This was certainly not always the case and in 1868 the filly Formosa won both Guineas races, the Oaks and the St Leger, a feat emulated in 1902 by Sceptre. Six fillies have won the Derby: Eleanor (1801), Blink Bonny (1857), Shotover (1882), Signorinetta (1908), Tagalie (1912) and Fifinella (1916).

Very few owners are willing to pit top-quality fillies against colts in Classic races today for financial reasons. With prizemoney levels for fillies-only events such as the 1,000 Guineas and Oaks in this country, not to mention their equivalent races in Ireland and France, almost as great and needing less exalted performances to win, there is little point in taking on the colts even with a sex allowance in the weights. But in 1975 the pugnacious Texan Nelson Bunker Hunt ignored convention by running his French-trained filly Nobiliary in the Derby at Epsom and was almost rewarded for his enterprise when she finished runner-up to Grundy, the first of subsequent champion jockey Pat Eddery's Derby winners.

The Guineas events, held at Newmarket in the

Above left: This portrait in oils of Admiral Rous hangs in the National Horseracing Museum.

Left: Lord George Bentinck who dominated the English Turf during the middle years of the 19th century.

Opposite: Admiral Rous, the Father of the Jockey Club.

Spring, are junior in historical terms to the other three Classics. The 2,000 Guineas was inaugurated in 1809, followed five years later by the 1,000 Guineas. To some extent the absolute eminence of the Classics has been diluted by such races as Ascot's King George VI and Queen Elizabeth Diamond Stakes and the Eclipse Stakes at Sandown Park but a Classic victory still commands huge and valuable respect for the winner's breeding potential. A Derby success, worthwhile in prize-money terms alone, carries a far larger hidden bonus. During the two-and-a-half minutes or so it takes to run the premier Classic over Epsom's switchback course the prospective value of the winning horse rises manyfold. A Derby hero today is likely to be worth in the region of £20 million the split second he passes the winning post. Commercial breeders are seeking a deal to syndicate such champions as international stallions within a matter of days and a high percentage of those horses who have landed this supreme race are hurried away to stud on the completion of their three-year-old season.

The dominance of North American stock, established during the immediate post-Second World War period and emphasized throughout the next three decades, is beginning to lessen. Although the great Bluegrass studs of Kentucky remain market leaders in the production of Thoroughbreds for the Northern Hemisphere, the United States no longer has a stranglehold. The recent and massive input of Arab money into European racing and breeding has established a reverse trend in this volatile business and it is no longer inevitable that winners of the great races in England, Ireland and France will be shipped across the Atlantic. If anything, the trans-Atlantic drift is beginning to reverse towards the Old World with such notable recent champions as Dancing Brave and Reference Point standing at Sheikh Mohammed's Dalham Hall Stud in Newmarket. The bloodstock world remains a long way short of achieving parity but the substantial investment of Arab money has already acted as a brake against wholesale export. A lasting benefit to European breeding may well be the ultimate result.

After three hundred years history seems to be repeating itself since it was the introduction into England of Arab stallions which first raised the standards of breeding. Just three horses from the Middle and Near East were responsible for the foundation of Thoroughbred production in the United Kingdom and, eventually, far beyond. The Byerley Turk, the Darley Arabian and the Godolphin Arabian are the forebears of all modern racehorses traced in line of descent on the male side of their family trees and, as befits the

creators of great dynasties, their own histories are steeped in rumour and romance.

The Byerley Turk was captured from the Turkish Army at Buda in 1687 by Captain Robert Byerley of County Durham who happened to be commanding a troop of horse in the army of the Duke of Lorraine during that long-forgotten skirmish. Two years later, by which time Byerley was a colonel in command of the Sixth Dragoon Guards, he rode the Turk at the Battle of the Boyne, his charger's speed at one point enabling him to escape encirclement by opposing cavalry. When sent to stud the Byerley Turk was not specially fashionable as a stallion but one of his sons, a horse named Jigg, produced Partner, the best racehorse of his day at Newmarket, and the male line became established when Partner's grandson Herod emerged as the greatest stallion in the second half of the 18th century. Herod sired the winners of more than a thousand races to become leading sire no fewer than eight times. He was grandsire of the Derby winners Sergeant, Aimwell and Waxy and of Paragon and Beningbrough, winners of the St Leger.

The Darley Arabian came from Syria, acquired by Thomas Darley, the English consul at Aleppo at the end of the 17th century. Some sources suggest Darley obtained the horse in

discharge for a debt but however he came by the animal, described by a contemporary as 'a bay horse of exquisite quality with a white blaze and three white feet', he lost no time in sending the Arabian home to his father at Aldby Park in Yorkshire. The Darley Arabian arrived in England as a four-year-old and spent the rest of his productive life at Aldby Park, remaining active as a stallion until he died at the age of 30. Hardly 15 hands high, he was a potent stallion whose influence for improving the breed was disproportionate to his stature and in siring Flying Childers, perhaps the first truly great racehorse, he achieved a measure of immortality.

Like the other members of racing's Holy Trinity, the Godolphin Arabian never raced and even his origin is open to question, some historians claiming he was not an Arabian at all but a Barb. But most authorities believe he was of Jilfan blood from the Yemen and was one of four horses presented to the King of France by the Bey of Tunis. What is established is that he passed into the ownership of Edward Coke of Longford Hall, Derbyshire. When Mr Coke died in 1733 he willed all his bloodstock, including this horse, to the Earl of Godolphin. Standing just 14 hands 3 inches, the Godolphin Arabian lived to be 29 years of age and stood at his

Queens of the Turf (top left). This oil by D. G. Giles depicts Signorina (left), dam of the remarkable Signorinetta, winner of both the Derby and Oaks of 1908, and Sceptre who, six years earlier, was victorious in no fewer than four Classics, missing a clean sweep when beaten into fourth place behind Ard Patrick in the Derby.

Above left: Dede Marks, curator of the National Horseracing Museum, shows the colours of the Duke of Westminster worn by Fred Archer when winning the 1886 Derby on Ormonde, one of the greatest horses of the 19th century.

A panoramic view of racing at Salisbury (above), one of England's most historic racecourses and once visited by Queen Elizabeth I.

Right: Merci! Fifteen times French champion jockey Yves Saint-Martin receives the traditional velvet cap from Levy Board chairman Lord Plummer after winning the 200th St Leger, the world's oldest-established Classic race, on Daniel Wildenstein's colt Crow.

owner's country seat, Gogmagog near Cambridge. There he was well patronized and sired the full brothers Lath and Cade out of the mare Roxana. Both were notable racehorses and the Godolphin Arabian's line has survived into the present century, represented outstandingly by the great American racer Man o' War.

23

SOURCES OF HORSES

The world's Thoroughbred production areas are well defined. Climatic and agricultural suitability place Australia and New Zealand, some parts of South America, notably The Argentine, the United States and Canada, England, Ireland, France and Germany as the major sources for breeding racehorses. The comparative ease of international jet aircraft travel has had the effect of shrinking distances between these far-flung equine centres of population so that it has become commonplace for animals to be conceived in one country, foaled in another, sold to race in a third location and perhaps be retired to stud in yet another.

Horse transportation has grown into a sophisticated business during the past 30 years or so and the international movement of horses for both racing and breeding purposes is now a daily occurrence. Aircraft have been modified to accommodate horses in comfort and loading and unloading procedures are slick and efficient. These comparatively recent developments in the techniques of horse transport combine to integrate racehorse dealing and have given rise to a new breed of expert—the international bloodstock agent. Many leading owners and breeders now employ agents, managers and advisers to help in the conduct of their businesses. Such experts were unnecessary in the more simplistic early days of the stud farm

Above: Karamita foaling at the Aga Khan's Sheshoon Stud on the Curragh, with the active assistance of Tom Tyrrell, the stud groom.

Above right: Just a few minutes have elapsed and both mother and offspring are doing well.

Right: A full year has passed as Tom Tyrrell singles out Karamita's son – by Shernazar – to admire in the paddock.

Previous page: Pegasus flying above Newmarket . . . the weather vane at Tattersalls Park Paddocks sales complex.

when opulent men of the leisured class maintained establishments well stocked with choice mares and bred to clearly-defined if limited bloodlines with little thought of commerce.

The continuation of established family lines with the stud owner keeping a paternal eye on his breeding charts and the animals under his care necessitated only a small staff of grooms. Veterinary techniques were imprecise at best and owed more to practical experience than science. The stud farms of 19th- and early 20th-century owner-breeders may have been tranquil but, judged by modern standards, were also haphazard and inefficient. Today, with pressure to produce commercially fashionable stock, sales ring potential is paramount and studs have become far more labour intensive. Studs in Kentucky have led the way in refining and streamlining such developments. So much so that some

more traditional European horsemen level the accusation of conveyor-belt production methods at some of the largest Bluegrass establishments, suggesting they come uncomfortably close to the factory farming of foals.

Certainly practices in Kentucky are formulated to provide the swiftest possible return on capital investment and it is difficult to escape the impression that horses are increasingly looked upon as a feature of the commodity market but, having said that, the standards of high-tech care are extraordinary. In some Kentucky studs all matings are video-recorded, veterinary departments with the latest equipment are to be found on site while specialist consultants and therapists boasting impressive qualifications form a vital element of the staff structure. Kentucky's super-efficient methods are not yet fully mirrored in Europe. The greatest disparity is in size. While the most palatial American farms house more than 20 stallions it is unusual to find a stud standing more than half-a-dozen on this side of the Atlantic.

Having visited a carefully-chosen stallion, mares normally return to their home paddock to await foaling. As with any new-born infant, a foal's first few hours of life require painstaking care and experienced staff should always be on hand to cope with any immediate post-natal crisis. But of equal importance, at least in strictly financial terms, is the care of young stock during the lead-up period to the major sales of yearlings. A smartly turned out and advantageously presented sales aspirant may fetch considerably more money at auction than one of comparable breeding and promise ill-prepared and poorly shown. But the buying of horses, like the breeding of them, is an infuriatingly imprecise science. Highly respected and richly rewarded experts have been known to advise their clients to part with huge sums for yearlings who subsequently

Previous page: Breeding mares at the Aga Khan's Ballymany Stud in County Kildare.

Right: Who said racing is a serious business? It's playtime for these foals at Dalham Hall Stud near Newmarket.

Below: Mares in a spacious paddock at the Whitsbury Manor Stud in Hampshire.

Opposite page: Breeders' Cup Turf heroine Pebbles with her foal by Derby winner Reference Point at foot.

A representative of successful stallion Rousillon's first crop, pictured in a paddock at the Side Hill Stud (right).

Below: Like father like son? Slip Anchor's first foal Anchor Light with his dam Doumayna at the Plantation Stud. Anchor Light is now in training with Henry Cecil.

proved useless as racehorses, while the fortunate few have purchased champions for a song.

Sales of yearling Thoroughbreds are held in all the world's principal breeding enclaves, most notably at Keeneland in the United States, at Newmarket, in Ireland and France. It is to these centres that leading figures in the bloodstock and racing industries make their way to replenish stocks and to engage in the business deals which oil the wheels of international horserac-

Right: David Elsworth in studious mood at the sales.

Yorkshire trainer Mel Brittain (centre right) thumbs his sales catalogue while studying the goods.

'Don't loose him, sir,' calls top auctioneer David Pim (far right). The man sales regulars nickname Pim's No. 1 is a brilliant rostrum performer.

The homely setting of Doncaster Bloodstock Sales (below), a popular venue for bargain hunters.

Irish experts sit ringside to appraise a prospect at Tattersalls' new sales complex at Fairhouse (below right).

ing. The level of excitement generated by public auctions of top-quality horseflesh must be experienced to be appreciated. The 'buzz' that affects the audience at a major bloodstock sale is perhaps comparable only to the hum of anticipation found at a Fine Art auction when a great Old Master canvas comes under the hammer.

The experienced bloodstock auctioneer will have a pretty accurate location for his serious bidders, being aware that only a handful of top owners or their agents are likely to be in the market for the choicest and hence costliest lots. At the premier yearling sales such as the Keeneland Select or the Tattersalls Highflyer only those with serious aspirations and bank balances to match will be bidding for the blue-blooded yearlings; before the sale commences their faces and preferred places around the ring will have been noted not only by the auctioneer himself but also by his 'spotters' whose task it is to draw the attention of the man with the hammer to the slightest twitch of interest from the right quarter.

Many yearlings are offered for sale with a reserve figure known only to the vendor and the auctioneer. Once bidding reaches the appropriate figure the auctioneer will announce that the yearling being offered is 'on the market and being sold'. Should the reserve not be attained, the lot will be led out unsold. The animal may be subject to a private sale outside the ring or be re-offered at a subsequent auction.

The bloodstock business is uncompromising and can be ruthless. It is certainly no place for the unwary amateur. Long before the actual public bidding occurs, hours of careful research

Left: A high-level sales discussion between Sheikh Mohammed (second left), his racing manager Anthony Stroud (wearing a cap) and trainers John Gosden (left) and Henry Cecil (right).

Below: An aerial view of Sheikh Hamdan Al-Maktoum's lavish new stud at Thetford in Norfolk, home of the stallions Nashwan, Unfuwain and Green Desert.

Below right: Wifely advice for bloodstock agent David Minton.

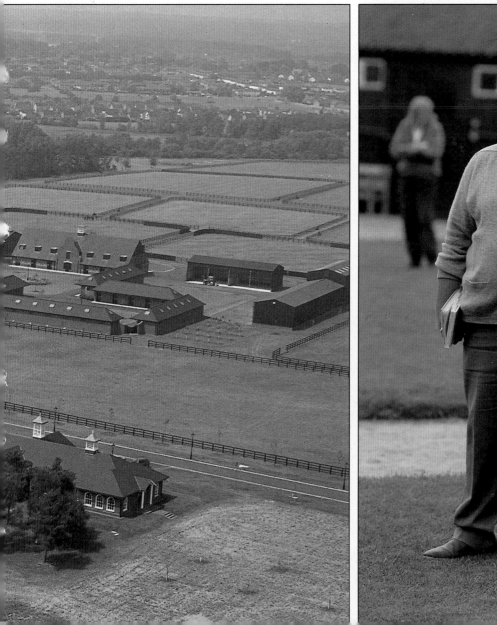

breeding industry is illustrated by the fact that in Britain and Ireland alone there are 850 studs feeding the needs of racing. Add to this remarkable figure the numerous outlets in such other European centres as France and West Germany plus the Americas, Australia and New Zealand and the rapidly growing Japanese market and it can readily be seen that the production of racehorses is a capital industry of world-wide significance. In terms of financial turnover, too, and therefore in international currency movements, bloodstock breeding and sales make a considerable impact. In such countries as Ireland, with her agricultural bias, the production of racehorses earns substantial and vital foreign currency.

The wealthiest of international racing's owners, such men as the Maktoum brothers from Dubai, Prince Khalid Abdullah from Saudi Arabia, HH The Aga Khan and Robert Sangster, have spread their Turf interests on a global level. Not only do their horses race in the majority of first-grade racing nations but their pattern of Thoroughbred studs has expanded to meet increasing needs. Robert Sangster, the only Englishman operating in this rarefied atmosphere of top international owner-breeders, was probably the first equine entrepreneur to envisage such multi-national methods and to put into practice his plan for a racing empire spanning both hemispheres. Sangster's influence is as high-profile in Australia, for example, as it is in Europe. He also races extensively in countries as diverse as the United States and South Africa. But if Sangster led the way, other members of the super league have lost no time in following suit and the Maktoums are now established in the United States and Australia. The Aga Khan and Prince Khalid also breed in America and race extensively there.

Of course, while such multi-millionaires lead the racing and breeding industries on both domestic and global planes, the bulk of Thoroughbred production for the middle market comes from altogether smaller and more modest operations—which is not to say less capable of producing good horses and the occasional champion. But let us look first at the high-powered production line of, as an example, Sheikh Mohammed Al-Maktoum's Dalham Hall Stud on the outskirts of Newmarket, home of such noted young stallions as the Derby-winning Ref-

will have been undertaken by highly-qualified experts in an attempt to identify the top prospects in terms of breeding and conformation. Many of the yearlings will have been seen by prospective buyers and their agents at the vending studs and only when armed with every available detail will bids worth hundreds of thousands be made.

The charting of pedigrees goes back many generations. A serious pedigree student will go to endless trouble before planning a covering or in attempting to assess the likely merit of an offspring. Such people are frequently employed by both commercial breeders and prospective purchasers. Just a handful of breeders who both sell and race their own products can claim to be holders of such intricate wisdom—Brigadier Gerard's owner-breeder John Hislop is one—but the majority need to have use of the services of people with this knowledge and experience when planning which stallions to use on their mares to obtain the best results. The greater the commercial basis of the operation, the greater the need for careful research at every stage of production.

The extent of the commercial Thoroughbred

erence Point and Dancing Brave, who numbered the Prix de l'Arc de Triomphe among his big-race victories.

Dalham Hall forms part of the international stud empire under the control of the Maktoum brothers. In addition to Dalham Hall, Sheikh Mohammed has the Derisley Wood, Hadrian and Rutland Studs also at Newmarket, and the

---

Previous page: Goffs spectacular sales ring at Kill in County Kildare, photographed during an evening session.

Left: Early one morning at Tattersalls Sales, Newmarket . . . and trainer Lord John FitzGerald.

Below: A pre-sales conference for board members of the British Bloodstock Agency: (Left to right) Sir Philip Payne-Gallwey, Bart., Jos. Collins, Major Christo Philipson (managing director) and Major Johnny Lewis.

Below, centre: Wiltshire trainer Richard Hannon, sporting a natty line in cardigans, pictured with Irish bloodstock expert Tim Hyde.

Below, far right: England goalkeeper Peter Shilton on the lookout for a yearling at Doncaster Bloodstock Sales with expert advice coming from Philip Mitchell, the Epsom trainer. Mitchell's wife Trish seems to have heard it all before.

Woodpark and Kildangan Studs in Ireland. Mohammed's elder brother Sheikh Maktoum Al-Maktoum owns the Gainsborough Stud in Berkshire and Gainsborough Farm, Kentucky. Sheikh Hamdan is associated with the Shadwell Stud complex in this country—the magnificent new Nunnery Stud at Thetford will be discussed later in this chapter—while in the United States his breeding interests are collectively known as Shadwell Farm. Additionally, Sheikh Hamdan owns the Derrinstown Stud in County Kildare, Ireland. Sheikh Ahmed, youngest of the Dubai racing dynasty, has Aston Upthorpe Stud in Oxfordshire where the stallions include his outstanding champion Mtoto.

Between them the Maktoums currently stand 25 stallions around the world. But Dalham Hall is the hub of their carefully planned and lavishly run breeding operation. Here stand the greatest of their highly valued stallions, covering specially selected mares always of good family and frequently of quality racecourse achievement in their own right. The days when Sheikh Mohammed and his brothers needed to break sales records in order to obtain top-of-the-market yearlings at public auction have all but passed into memory as the Arabs increasingly

breed their own potential champions, often exclusively from their own stock.

Acting under the umbrella of Darley Stud Management Company Limited, the Maktoums increase their stake in racing and breeding on an annual basis. As soon as one set of statistics is published it becomes outdated. But at the last count of horses in training, stallions, mares, foals and so on, the Al-Maktoums controlled an equine population of some 1,500 Thoroughbreds.

Hamdan, with nearly 300 in training in England, Ireland, the United States and Australia, has recently completed the building of the Nunnery Stud which extends over 500 acres (202 hectares) of prime Norfolk countryside and will house six stallions when in full production. Former champion European sprinter Green Desert is already a resident and was joined late in 1989 by Unfuwain and Nashwan. Limitless financial resources enabled the Nunnery Stud to be completed in little more than two years from blueprint. Every modern requirement is included and the level of craftmanship throughout makes this new establishment an outstanding example of just how a stud should be built and equipped. Four years in planning, the Nunnery Stud began

43

to be constructed only after the most extensive consultations between architects, management consultants, veterinary advisers, the stallion manager and other key personnel. Sheikh Hamdan himself paid great attention to design and layout with particular reference to adequate ventilation. Levels of winter heating and summer air conditioning are carefully suited to the climate of rural Norfolk.

The Nunnery, a curious name considering its primary function, centres around an area which includes office accommodation, the superb and spacious stallion complex, the covering shed and an indoor exercise unit. Some way distant are yards which include the foaling rooms and further back are looseboxes and American barns, totalling some 230 units in all. There is also an isolation yard for the use of mares coming from overseas and who require a period of quarantine. By using traditional, individually

Coolmore Stud in the Golden Vale of Tipperary (left) with a mare and her foal enjoying the lush Irish grass.

The splendidly-appointed Gainsborough Stud near Newbury (below left).

A champion in silhouette (below): Rainbow Quest at the Juddmonte Stud in Berkshire.

ventilated looseboxes to house both in-foal mares and mares with foals at foot, any risk of cross-infection should be minimized. In addition to the normal paddocks for mares and foals, the Nunnery boasts no fewer than twelve stallion paddocks, six with field shelters for summer use and a similar number closer to the stallion yard for the winter. The water supply for the whole stud comes from a borehole dropped into the chalk basin that provides water devoid of the additives normally found in mains supply. Such attention to detail is the hallmark of all the Al-Maktoum family's establishments.

Senior stud groom Bill Cornish, formerly at the Egerton and Lordship Studs in Newmarket, has been at Thetford since 1985 and is delighted by his working conditions there. 'The Nunnery Stud is magnificently appointed with every pos-

sible device for making the job of producing high-quality stock less hazardous,' he says. 'I cannot imagine better conditions to work under and when we get our full complement of six stallions the Nunnery should become not only a showplace but a great working stud as well.'

Twenty miles west along the A11 trunk road towards the outskirts of Newmarket we can discover a far smaller, more traditional stud with a comparable eye for detail and excellence. The Side Hill Stud, owned by Jockey Club Senior Steward the Marquess of Hartington and managed by John Warren, stands former top-class miler-cum-sprinter Chief Singer and Salse who won a string of good races in the maroon and white silks of Sheikh Mohammed. Side Hill became a public stud 60 years ago and among the top stallions to stand at this 140-acre complex was top sire Sharpen Up who went there on his retirement from the racecourse in 1973 and stayed until sold to the United States seven years later. In 1985 an extensive building programme, including a 30-stall American barn, a new foaling unit and offices, greatly increased the potential of Side Hill, which keeps half-a-dozen mares

Previous page: Viewing by floodlight at the Newmarket December Sales.

Left: Kris photographed at his lordly domain, the Thornton Stud near Thirsk.

Mares and foals at the Cheveley Park Stud, Newmarket.

permanently on site in addition to boarders. The outlook of this small but efficient operation is modern and commercial, the Stud normally selling at the Tattersalls Highflyer, October and December Sales staged at nearby Park Paddocks.

Among the many breeding establishments located in and around Newmarket is the National Stud itself, to be found at the eastern end of the town and adjoining the July Racecourse. Geographically speaking, the National Stud has had a somewhat chequered background. Curious though it may seem, the English National Stud was founded in Ireland when, in 1916, Lord Wavertree presented to the nation his estate at Tully in Co. Kildare on the understanding that the government would appoint a manager dedicated to the breeding of the highest class of racehorse. The Wavertree stud contained 43 mares at that time including representatives of some outstanding bloodlines and was maintained successfully as a commercial enterprise. Potentially top-quality colts and fillies were later leased to race in the colours of King George VI and the present Queen. But by the time Elizabeth II had come to the throne, the National Stud had moved home twice.

In 1943 Tully was handed over to the Irish government and took on the title of the Irish National Stud with stock belonging to the previous management shipped over to Gillingham in Dorset. Big Game, the National Stud's star stallion came too even though there was great uncertainty over the future of racing in those dark and dismal wartime days. In 1949, with a far more hopeful climate, the National Stud moved again, this time to West Grinstead in Sussex, where it was possible to provide extra accommodation. But a more radical change followed in 1963 when a new objective, that of keeping stallions in England for the benefit of home-based breeders, was undertaken. Gillingham, now surplus to requirements, was sold and partly with this money the new National Stud on the out-

Right: To buy or not to buy? John Magnier, Vincent O'Brien and Tommy Stack give full attention at a session of Goffs' Yearling Sales in Ireland.

Below: Eyeing up the merchandise . . . former Beckhampton trainer Jeremy Tree, racing manager Grant Pritchard-Gordon and Prince Khalid Abdullah among assessors at a session of the Newmarket Highflyer Sales.

Below right: Mana Al-Maktoum (third left) and his cousin Maktoum Al-Maktoum view a yearling at Park Paddocks, Newmarket.

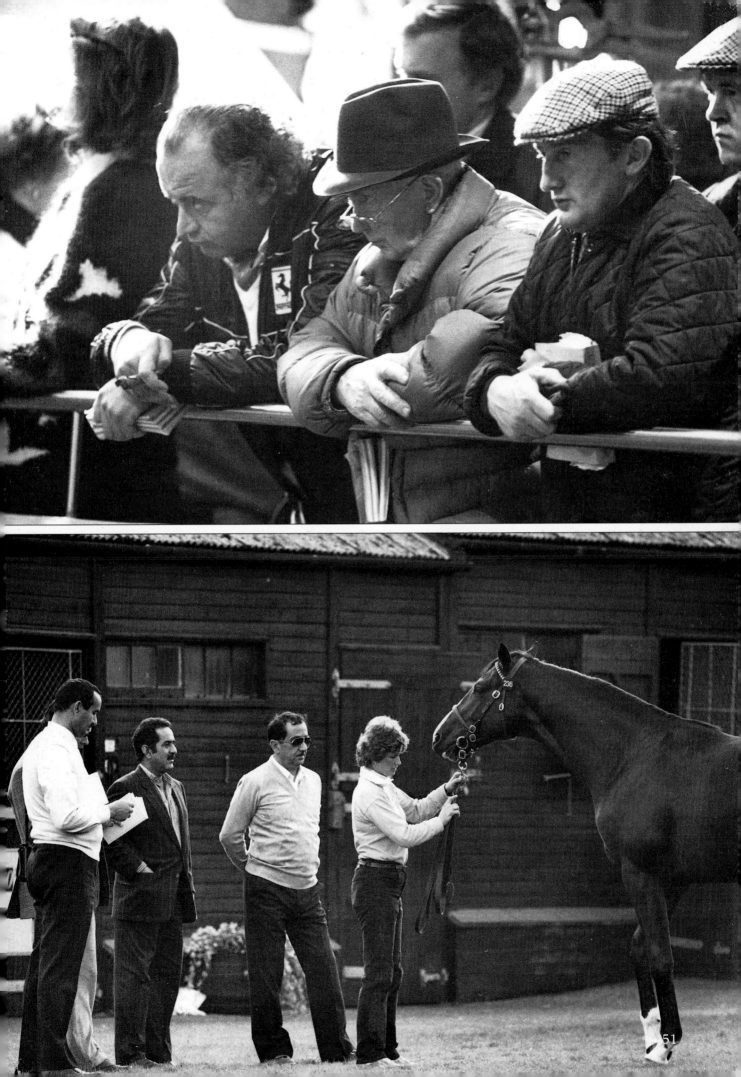

MILL REEF

Bay Horse 1968-1986

By Never Bend out of Milan Mill by Princequillo.

Winner of The Derby, The Eclipse, The King George VI and
Queen Elizabeth Stakes and The Prix de L'Arc de Triomphe.

Bred and owned by Paul Mellon, Rokeby Farms, Upperville, Virginia.

Trained by Ian Balding, Kingsclere. Ridden by Geoff Lewis.

Stood at National Stud 1973 - 1986, Leading Sire 1978.

His Companion at Kingsclere, John Hallum.

His Companion at National Stud, George Roth.

John Skeaping R.A. Sculptor.

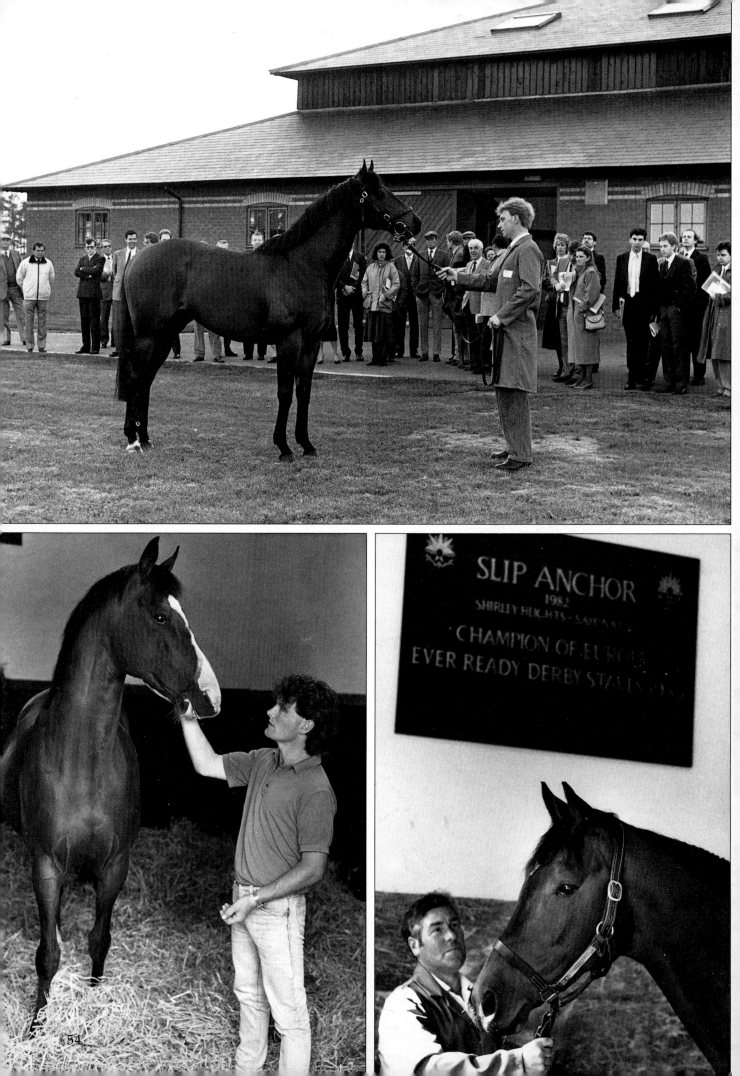

SLIP ANCHOR
1982
SHIRLEY HEIGHTS – SAYONARA

CHAMPION OF EUROPE
EVER READY DERBY STAKES 1985

Previous page: Walking the stallions at Newmarket's National Stud with the memorial to the great Mill Reef in the foreground.

Salse (left) takes a keen interest in the passing scene from his box at the Side Hill Stud.

Far left: Green Desert, first resident stallion at Sheikh Hamdan Al-Maktoum's magnificent Nunnery Stud in Norfolk, strikes a pose for an admiring group of visitors.

Fashionable and successful young Coolmore stallion Sadler's Wells looking regal with a proud Paul Gleeson at his head (below, far left).

Below centre: Slip Anchor, Lord Howard de Walden's 1985 Ever Ready Derby winner, by a plaque proclaiming his illustrious status.

A crisp winter morning at Dalham Hall with Shareef Dancer (below) leading the parade of Al-Maktoum stallions.

skirts of Newmarket was built, at that time boasting the most modern and best equipped facilities anywhere in the breeding world.

West Grinstead was disposed of in 1972 and at last the entire operation centred at the Stud's new headquarters. The National Stud holds shares in the stallions standing there with nominations allocated by ballot to breeders who apply. Without question, the National Stud's greatest asset in recent times was the Derby and Prix de l'Arc de Triomphe winner of 1971, Mill Reef, who went on to prove himself as great a stallion (champion sire in 1978 and 1987) as he had been a star on the racecourse; the decision of his American owner-breeder, Paul Mellon, to allow Mill Reef to stand in this country was a sign of singular friendship and philanthropy. Never Say Die and Blakeney are other Derby winners to have acted as National Stud stallions. The establishment is now the responsibility of the statutory Horserace Betting Levy Board which administers the Stud's finances without seeking to impose on its breeding policies or its separate identity.

Her Majesty the Queen is, judged by the most exacting standards, a Thoroughbred breeding expert and her day-to-day interest in the Royal Studs a vital part of her great patronage of British racing. There has been a Royal Stud since the days of King Henry VIII when mares and foals were kept at Hampton Court Palace, then occupying a more placid and rural Thames-side aspect than today. Perhaps Edward VII displayed more than a touch of clairvoyance when he settled on Sandringham in Norfolk as a relocation and it is there that the Queen stands the 1978 Derby and Irish Derby hero Shirley Heights and Bustino, the 1974 St Leger winner, both now influential and popular sires.

Products of the Royal Studs have won nearly 50 European Group I events; they include the 1985 Derby victor Slip Anchor (by Shirley Heights) and the Queen's fine fillies Highclere (1,000 Guineas and Prix de Diane) and Dunfermline (Oaks and St Leger). But such is the historic success of the Royal Studs that even these Classic triumphs are really no more than a continuation of excellence. After all, the mighty Eclipse himself, 'allowed by all ranks of sportsmen to be the fleetest horse that ever ran' according to Whyte's *History of the British Turf,* came from the then Royal Stud in Windsor Forest and no fewer than seven Derby winners have followed in his peerless hoofprints.

Breeding, racing and the Monarchy have been entwined across the centuries although not all the Queen's predecessors demonstrated the same knowledge and enthusiasm as she. Some looked upon the Royal Studs with no more than a passing nod to duty while others rushed headlong into a business they did not fully understand. The present decade's success story at the Royal Studs says much for the steady hand on the tiller and the expert personal interest of the Queen.

TRAINERS

The difficult and exacting craft of training the horse is as old as racing itself but has grown in sophistication and complexity during the past quarter-century as never before. From one training establishment to another methods have, of course, always varied but many of the 'absolute truths' adhered to as recently as the 19th century would now be heresy to contemporary racehorse trainers. It was, for example, commonplace at one time for trainers to attempt rapid fitness by subjecting their horses to a method known as sweating which involved individuals being galloped long distances clad in an array of sheets and blankets. This drastic system caused horses to lose weight instantaneously and, provided they survived the regime, no doubt put an edge on their condition. Now, thankfully, trainers favour a more gradual programme to achieve the same ends and, indeed, contemporary horsemasters are far less severe than their predecessors in preparing horses for the racecourse and keeping them at a peak of excellence and physical condition.

As with so many disciplines in connection with the horse, training is an imprecise science. No two trainers follow exactly the same formula and, in any case, no two horses respond in identical fashion. Thus trial and error must be resorted to. Frequent fast work over sprint distances may bring one horse to racing fitness while another of similar breeding and confirmation will require a more patient approach, perhaps involving half-speed work on an uphill gallop to achieve a similar state of readiness.

Timing of preparation is all important. You will sometimes hear it said of a trainer that he is able to produce fanced runners 'ready to the minute'. There is no higher praise for a top professional. But just how such perfection is reached will vary from one yard to another to a greater or lesser degree.

The modern trainer needs to be multi-talented. In the highly developed commercial world of today's racing industry it is no longer enough for a trainer to understand horses alone. Of course that remains fundamental to the job but the successful present-day stableman also needs administrative and marketing skills, a well-developed public relations image and the knowledge to make use of a baffling array of sec-

retarial software (or the income to pay a salary for someone else to work the computer and word processor). The training of racehorses is a 365-day-a-year occupation and not, contrary to some sections of public opinion, a soft option. A genuine love of horses is a prerequisite and so is the capacity for working long hours, the patience to combat everyday frustrations and an overall dedication.

The British Isles currently boasts a crop of outstanding trainers who bear comparison with any in the world. The arbitrary composition of any selection of great training names and their

Previous page: Dawn on the Curragh. Members of the Kevin Prendergast team pull out for exercise.

John Dunlop (right), the distinguished Arundel trainer. Below left: Let's hope the water is warm. Trainer Clive Brittain supervising swimming exercise for one of his Newmarket string.

Below: Post-race conference in the winners' enclosure at Newbury between Angus Gold, Hamdan Al-Maktoum's racing manager, jockey Willie Carson and trainer Dick Hern.

Lady Herries (left), who trains at Angmering on the Sussex coast.

Conversation piece (bottom). Leading trainers Henry Cecil, on the grey, and Michael Stoute talking shop.

Below: Training brothers Ian and Toby Balding.

Opposite page: John Gosden (top right) moved from Southern California to Newmarket in 1989.

Whatcombe trainer Paul Cole (centre right).

Below right: South African jockey Michael Roberts leading a typical convoy at Newmarket, Britain's largest training centre.

stables must be subjective and open to amendment by other individuals. Certainly, this is not an attempt to make a definitive or absolute 'order of merit' and it is strictly an alphabetical list of some of the modern exponents of the training art.

Jack Berry combines training with farming interests on the Lancashire coast at Cockerham. Now aged 52, he has been training for 20 years, gradually building a highly successful and widely respected stable in what might be considered a racing outpost. A specialist at selecting and preparing speed horses, particularly juveniles, Jack Berry has helped restore pride to the North of England racing community. A highly practical man assisted by his wife Jo and sons, he knows the limitations of the animals at his disposal and rarely mistakes the proper opportunities for the horses in his charge. A fine stableman in addition to being a most able trainer—these attributes are not necessarily synonymous—his horses always look a picture and stand up well to their racing as an ever-increasing number of winners demonstrates. A keen eye for potential at the yearling sales and painstaking professionalism are hallmarks of the Berry system—as well

as a hint of superstition. He is never seen at the races without his lucky red shirt, even when in top hat and tails for Royal Ascot.

Henry Cecil has won the Derby twice, with Slip Anchor in 1985 and Reference Point two years later, every other Classic more than once together with nearly every major Group race on the calendar. He has landed the trainers' championship no fewer than eight times since 1976, and in 1987 trained a British record 180 winners, surpassing John Day's 1846 total.

The urbane, engagingly eccentric Henry Richard Amherst Cecil followed his father-in-law, Sir Noel Murless, as master of the famous Warren Place yard at Newmarket and has fully maintained the exceptional standards of that great establishment. From the start of his training career in 1969, following four years as assistant to the redoubtable Sir Cecil Boyd-Rochfort, his step-father, Henry Cecil has handled top horses for top people. But his position as leader of his craft is only perpetuated by the production of a never-ending stream of high-quality winners, a state of affairs he seems able to continue with almost deceptive ease. He has an uncanny instinct for when a horse is 'right'—ready to win. He prefers to rely on that instinct than the battery of scientific analyses now available to modern trainers.

Classic race winners are never in short supply at Warren Place but the tall, slim, slightly ingenuous Cecil no longer needs to prove his outstanding abilities. Relaxing over a cup of Earl Grey in his drawing room—he is addicted to tea—or strolling in his celebrated and beautiful rose garden, he might be almost anything but a champion trainer of champion racehorses. Never seen with binoculars, rarely wearing a hat and sometimes startling his more conventional peers by going racing in lurid golf slacks, Cecil is

Right: The appearance of ease . . . Jeremy Tree retired from training at the conclusion of the 1989 Flat-racing season.

Below left: Pulborough trainer Guy Harwood (right) with a vital member of his backroom staff, stable vet Brian Ingles.

Right turn . . . Luca Cumani (below), the Italian who trains with great success at Newmarket.

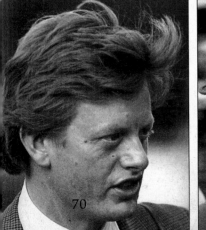

William Jarvis (above), latest member of a Newmarket training dynasty.

Paul Kelleway in typically pugnacious pose (left).

Alec Stewart (below, extreme left), the successful young Newmarket trainer.

Geoff Wragg (below left), a leading Newmarket trainer, caught in thoughtful mood.

Previous page: Top miler Warning heads the Guy Harwood string on an autumn morning.

certainly unconventional but his record proclaims total mastery of his exacting business.

In contrast to Cecil, **John Dunlop** has no background in professional racing, being the son of a country doctor. But in the early 1960s he applied for the post of assistant to Neville Dent and later took up a similar appointment with Gordon Smyth at the Castle Stables, Arundel. In 1966, at the age of only 27, Dunlop took over the Arundel licence, soon opening up this historic yard to the public ownership of horses in a yard formerly used as a private establishment for the Duke and Duchess of Norfolk and a handful of family friends.

Dunlop's laid-back public image tends to disguise one of racing's keenest brains. The huge

David Elsworth (above), a man for all seasons. The Hampshire trainer saddled 54 winners during the 1988–89 National Hunt season and followed up with a further 35 on the Flat to earn his patrons £800,000 in little more than a calendar year.

William Haggas (above right), the young Newmarket trainer.

Thanks, mate! Ebullient trainer Ron Boss (right) is clearly grateful that his colt Balla Cove has just won the Tattersalls Middle Park Stakes.

Alex Scott (below right). He enjoyed a fine first season training at Newmarket in 1989.

Newmarket's Ben Hanbury (below, far right) must have just saddled a winner!

Sussex stable under his care is run on commercial, modern methods with endless care expended on placing horses to their best advantage. His skill in improving horses after their first run is well known in the game. His record of winning top events in Europe and beyond is unmatched by any contemporary trainer and his ability to plunder big prizes in Italy and West Germany in particular is the envy of many of his rivals. In 1987, for example, he saddled the winners of 61 races worth £403,000 in this country but during the same period won for his patrons

Previous page: Henry Cecil's Warren Place string, stretching as far as the eye can see.

Left: Epsom's Brooke Sanders, pictured with Calapaez.

Peter Hudson (below), trainer of the speedy Pharaoh's Delight.

Richard Hannon (bottom) studies the next day's opposition with the aid of Raceform.

Lambourn trainer Peter Walwyn (right).

Below right: Lambourn trainer Charlie Nelson issues work routine instructions to jockey John Reid.

no less than £603,000 overseas. Nor is this an isolated set of figures. This international success brings in income in Japanese yen and Australian dollars apart from more familiar European currencies but his home operation is equally successful and among his Classic winners was Shirley Heights in the 1978 Derby.

Yorkshire grit and horsesense is personified by the Malton trainer **Peter Easterby** who operates on an all-year-round basis and produces his fair share of winners with the regularity of a true professional. Easterby, whose real names are Miles Henry, has always been known as Peter to differentiate him from his trainer brother Mick (M.W.). He first took out a licence in 1950 and the majority of his early wins were with jumpers. He has saddled the winners of no fewer than five Champion Hurdles and two Cheltenham Gold Cups. But he has proved equally adept at producing Flat winners, too, and numbers the Ladbroke Chester Cup (twice), the Ebor and the Lincoln Handicaps among his summer-season successes. His raids on southern tracks are always to be feared. A tough Yorkshireman who tends to look upon anyone living—and training—south of the Wash as a bit soft, Peter Easterby has proved the efficacy of his methods for nearly 40 years.

A man for all seasons, **David Elsworth** handles a large mixed string at his stables in Hampshire, setting a comprehensive standard of excellence by saddling Group winners on the Flat in addition to having won, in recent seasons, the two greatest steeplechases. He sent out Rhyme 'N' Reason to win the Seagram Grand National in 1988 and Desert Orchid triumphed for him in the 1989 Cheltenham Gold Cup. At 50, Elsworth should have a long career still ahead of him and can be expected to add Classic victories on the Flat to the jumping achievements which have established him as a trainer of unusual merit. Methods of training slow-maturing National Hunt horses and more precocious Flat-race animals vary greatly, but David Elsworth has proved himself to be a master practitioner in both crafts.

Previous page: Working 'against the collar' on the all-weather track at Manton

Below: 'General' Barry Hills reviewing his cavalry at Manton.

Left: A decent length of leg and a comfortable hunting saddle – Barry Hills and his splendid hack make a fine picture on the Wiltshire Downs.

John Dunlop's Sussex neighbour and rival, **Guy Harwood** has also adopted an international stance throughout his career as a top-class trainer, bidding for the rich pickings in Europe, the United States and beyond. A master of his craft, Harwood keeps the members of his large and select string at Pulborough in American-style open barns rather than the traditional stable boxes still favoured by many British and European trainers.

He has done particularly well with horses owned by Prince Khalid Abdullah, winning the 1986 Prix de l'Arc de Triomphe with Dancing Brave who rates as one of the world's top middle-distance colts in recent years. Dancing Brave should also have landed that season's Derby but his late challenge was mistimed and he failed by just half a length to catch the Aga Khan's Shahrastani. Dancing Brave underlined his superiority by gaining revenge in both Ascot's King George VI and Queen Elizabeth Diamond Stakes and the Arc. He also won the 2,000 Guineas and the Eclipse Stakes in a *tour de force* which earned him comparison with such international stars as Nijinsky and Mill Reef. Sadly his racecourse career ended in disappointment and anticlimax when he could finish only fourth in the Breeders' Cup Turf at Santa Anita in California. Dancing Brave now stands as a stallion at Newmarket's Dalham Hall Stud, a great credit to his trainer.

More recently, Harwood has handled top miler Warning, also owned by Prince Khalid, and that redoubtable stayer Sadeem, twice a winner of the Ascot Gold Cup for Sheikh Mohammed. But the hallmark of the Pulborough method is that every horse in the yard is treated with exceptional care, whether a champion or a modest handicapper. Indeed, he has proved adept at placing unexposed horses with little public form to win the big handicaps, to the trepidation of the bookies.

Harwood insists on the welfare of his horses as a first priority, employs top-class stable staff and provides on-the-spot veterinary care of the highest order. This painstaking approach and eye for detail combine to make him one of England's best and most respected trainers.

Veteran trainer **Dick Hern** is a man of quite exceptional ability and great personal courage. At a time when many would have been considering retirement, he broke his neck in a hunting accident which resulted in his confinement to a wheelchair. Heart surgery followed and it seemed Hern's distinguished career was at an end. In fact, the golden autumn was yet to come. 'The Major', as he is known throughout the Turf community, produced Nashwan to win the 1989 2,000 Guineas, Derby, Eclipse and King George in a magnificent sequence that redoubled the affection in which this great trainer is held.

W. R. Hern's long career—he first held a training licence in 1957—has seen him handle many of the best horses of the post-war era including the previous Derby winners Troy and Henbit. But perhaps the only earlier inmate of his West Ilsley stable to stand comparison with Nashwan was Brigadier Gerard who carried off 17 races from five furlongs to a mile and a half and was beaten only once, by the Derby winner Roberto, during a career which established him as a racehorse of unusual merit. Hern's handling of Brigadier Gerard was exemplary and reflected great credit on his skill and consideration for the champion colt, one of only two horses to master Mill Reef when he gained the measure of Ian Balding's star in the 1971 2,000 Guineas. Unlike Mill Reef, Brigadier Gerard gained little distinction as a sire but there is no questioning his outstanding ability on the racecourse.

Hern has had numerous triumphs with horses owned by the Queen, the owner of the West Ilsley yard, notably the Classic winners Dunfermline and Highclere. His record of nurturing top-quality horses stands comparison with any trainer at least of modern times and the

way in which he fostered Nashwan's abilities marks him as a true master of his craft.

Lady Anne Herries, who trains a small, mixed string at Angmering Park in West Sussex, is a comparative newcomer to the ranks of trainers but has been brought up with racehorses since both her late father, the Duke of Norfolk, and her mother, Lavinia, Duchess of Norfolk, always kept animals in training with Willie and Gordon Smyth and John Dunlop at Arundel. She is a skilled placer of her horses, and her winners are usually well-backed. Lady Herries has done particularly well with her mother's grey colt Sheriff's Star, winner of the Coronation Cup (Group I) at Epsom and the Grand Prix de Saint-Cloud (Group I) during 1989.

High on the Downs above Marlborough in Wiltshire stands the fabled training centre of Manton, now home base for **Barry Hills** and his

Right: Out in the meadow, a misty start at Richard Whitaker's Yorkshire stable.

Nigel Tinker's horses return home from the gallops (below).

Scottish trainer John Wilson's string paddle on a peaceful Ayrshire beach (below right).

string of highly-bred racehorses. Hills, small and dapper, moved there from Lambourn a few years ago to take over from former National Hunt trainer Michael Dickinson who had been hired by Robert Sangster to rebuild this historic but derelict yard. After a brief but traumatic stay Dickinson continued his career in America but his successor is reaping the benefits of all the meticulous planning and huge investment. Manton is back in the forefront of British racing although Robert Sangster put the great training centre back on the market in late 1989 at an asking price of £15 million.

Barry Hills calls Manton 'the perfect place to train good racehorses' and anyone who has seen the magnificently equipped establishment and the variety of gallops, set in a splendid and peaceful environment, could hardly disagree with that view.

Hills learned his craft the hard way as jockey, stableman, form expert and gambler. He won enough money punting to try his hand at training and has never looked back. Now he operates at the top end of the business, training for such owners as Sangster, Khalid Abdullah and Sheikh Mohammed. Although he has yet to win the Derby, Hills has saddled the winners of almost all Europe's other top events including the Prix de l'Arc de Triomphe, the Budweiser Irish Derby, the Irish Oaks, both 1,000 and 2,000 Guineas, two Ascot Gold Cups, two Benson and Hedges Gold Cups and two Grand Prix de Saint-Cloud. He is also head of a rapidly forming Turf dynasty, his son John having taken over the old family stable at South Bank in Lambourn while twin brothers Michael and Richard are both successful jockeys, the former under contract to his father at Manton and the latter riding for Tom Jones's stable at Newmarket.

Keen-eyed and experienced, **Reg Hollinshead** trains away from the racing mainstream at Rugeley in Staffordshire where his mixed string can be expected to win races throughout the year. Hollinshead, who rode as both an amateur and a professional as a young man, is also noted as a fine 'schoolmaster' of young jockeys. Tony Ives, Kevin Darley and Dean McKeown are among the successful riders who owe much to

Above left: Jack Berry and stable favourite O. I. Oyston pictured by the 'phone box alongside the all-weather gallop. Hoping for the early prices from Ladbrokes?

Left: Marlborough trainer Peter Makin watches his string at exercise on the Wiltshire Downs.

Working on a wet morning. Reg Hollinshead's all-weather training track at Upper Longdon (above right).

Right: Yorkshire's David Chapman with his outstanding sprint handicapper Chaplin's Club.

his tutelage. A good all-rounder who also farms and runs his own small stud, Reg Hollinshead and other trainers like him form the backbone of their profession.

One of the small band of women riders who first rode against men in this country, **Brooke Sanders** now has a yard at Epsom, training both jumpers and Flat horses. She is not operating at the fashionable end of the market but her horses always look well and run to the limit of their capabilities. It may yet be some time before women Flat-race trainers in England do as well as Jenny Pitman, Mercy Rimell and Monica Dickinson have under National Hunt Rules or, indeed, produce major race winners like Criquette Head has done in France, but this is down to lack of patronage rather than lack of

Previous page: Horses working on Epsom Downs with the grandstand in the background.

Above right: A tip from the master. Staffordshire trainer Reg Hollinshead offers advice to his apprentice Tony Culhane.
Lynda Ramsden (right) who trains near Thirsk in North Yorkshire.
Below: Richmond, Yorkshire trainer Bill Watts watches members of his team return from exercise.

ability. Miss Sanders, hard-working and talented, is more likely than most to make the breakthrough. She saddled Double Dutch to win the 1989 Cesarewitch.

Scottish-born **Alec Stewart** became a public trainer as recently as the start of the 1983 Flat-racing season but has gone to the top in a very short while. He acted as assistant to Gavin Hunter and Tom Jones for a total of six years before that, however, so clearly knows his craft.

One good horse can sometimes make a young trainer's name almost overnight and in the case of Alec Stewart that horse was Mtoto, winner of the Eclipse Stakes in both 1987 and 1988 and the first horse to land Sandown's great race back-to-back since Polyphontes in the 1920s. Stewart's champion also won the 1988 King George VI and Queen Elizabeth Diamond Stakes. Mtoto

Above left: No butts about it: stable goat Gina gets her marching orders from trainer John Wilson.

Bill Wightman (left) has held a training licence for more than fifty years.

Richard Whitaker (extreme left), whose Wetherby yard has become a major force in recent years.

Below: John Wilson's well-behaved string from Cree Lodge look unworried by rush-hour traffic in Ayr.

Above: A unique Mark Cranham picture of Sheikh Mohammed, Europe's leading owner, riding out at Newmarket. The Sheikh (second right) is accompanied by (right to left) veteran jockey Greville Starkey, racing manager Anthony Stroud and trainer Michael Stoute. Pulling out at the Freemason Lodge Stables of champion trainer Michael Stoute (above right).

Right: Dave Kitcher with the filly Salsabil on a driving rein at Arundel in November 1988. Eleven months later Salsabil won the Prix Marcel Boussac at Longchamp.

then came within inches of taking the Arc but his run came just too late to catch the Italian five-year-old Tony Bin.

Stewart had, however, proved his ability when saddling Opale to score in the Irish St Leger when in only his second season of training. Careful not to over-race his horses, Alec Stewart is a thoughtful young man with high ambitions and the skills to match them. He looks set to become a master trainer in the years to come.

The description 'master trainer' already applies to Barbados-born **Michael Stoute**, 10 years Stewart's senior. Son of the island's police chief, Stoute was determined to get into racing on whatever level. At one time he thought of trying to become a journalist or broadcaster and 'tested' for BBC Television. But it was the training of racehorses rather than speaking about them which proved to be Stoute's forte.

Having first taken a job as pupil-assistant with Yorkshire-based Irish trainer Pat Rohan, Stoute arrived in Newmarket to take up a similar position with the late Douglas Smith in 1968. Two years later he moved to join Tom Jones—how often that name comes up as mentor of would-be

trainers!—and took out a training licence in 1972. It did not take Stoute, a keen and knowledgeable cricket fan, long to start scoring some racing 'runs'. Now his record stands comparison with any other present-day trainer, including Derby triumphs with Shergar (1981) and Shahrastani (1986). His other Classic credits include a trio of Irish Derbys, the 1,000 and 2,000 Guineas in both this country and Ireland and three Epsom and Curragh Oaks. His runners have also taken the 'King George', Goodwood's Sussex Stakes, the Ascot Gold Cup and two July Cups.

In fact, it is more difficult to find major races the Beech Hurst stable has not collected than those it has. Stoute's great record shows him to be a trainer of outstanding merit and his ability to get the best out of fillies is acknowledged throughout the Turf community. Still a young man, Michael Stoute should continue to rewrite the record books for many years to come. Quite a loss to the racing media world . . .

The Yorkshire training centre at Middleham has long housed good horses and high-grade trainers. **Chris Thornton** maintains a tradition there having received his grounding in the business with Sam Armstrong, father of the Newmarket trainer Robert and father-in-law of Lester Pigott, Theo Greiper in Germany and finally with Sam Hall, one of Middleham's finest trainers.

Thornton is well known as a perfectionist and a keen student of the form book who always places his horses to the best possible advantage. He has done particularly well with the ultra-consistent Apache in recent seasons. His horses should always be noted at Ayr for he has an outstanding record on Scotland's premier track. York has also proved a happy hunting ground for Thornton's elegant Spigot Lodge yard over the years.

The Master of Beckhampton, **Jeremy Tree** retired at the conclusion of the 1989 season, handing over his famous stable to long-serving

assistant Roger Charlton. Tree trained horses from March 1952 with all the care, concern and professionalism of a master. Rotund of build and often to be seen puffing reflectively on a cigarette in an elegant holder, he may not appear a typical member of his profession. But he knows just about all there is to know of horses and what makes them reach a peak of racecourse fitness.

During those 37 years of his career he turned out a regular stream of top-class animals (among them Juliette Marny, Sharpo and Rainbow Quest), winning a handful of Classics, the Arc and many other important events. The patrons of Beckhampton, among them Prince Khalid

Chris Thornton (right), the Middleham trainer, watching work.
Below: Chris Thornton's team pictured against the magnificent backdrop of Lord Bolton's Estate in the Yorkshire Dales.
Stable work is never done. A hurrying lass at Chris Thornton's Yorkshire yard (below right).

Abdullah, received exceptional service from Tree who says he 'intends to go on interfering' at the stable during his retirement. No doubt Roger Charlton will be grateful for that.

After learning his job while acting as assistant to his Newmarket-based father Jack, **Bill Watts** moved to Richmond in Yorkshire 20 years ago and has become the leading North-country trainer. His credits include landing the Budweiser Arlington Million in America with Lord Derby's horse Teleprompter in 1985 and the 1,000 Guineas success of Waterloo. Watts has also proved himself to be a fine placer of top handicappers with victories in such highly competitive events as the Royal Hunt Cup at Royal Ascot, the William Hill Gold Cup and the Bunbury Cup (twice). Ireland's Pacemaker International has also fallen twice to his stable as has Ascot's Queen Alexandra Stakes.

Much respected on the northern and Scottish circuits, the Watts runners command special attention when he decides to raid the major southern courses. Representative of a long-established training family, Bill Watts continues to set the standard north of the Trent.

The lush, green pastures of Ireland, many of which have never been subjected to the plough, provide ideal locations for the breeding and training of the racehorse. So extensive is the rearing of the Thoroughbred in this lovely island nation that the Irish economy is dependent on the twin industries of racehorse production and husbandry to an unusual degree even among comparable agriculture-based countries. Ireland is, of course, the primary source of National Hunt stock but her ability to provide high-quality Flat horses is almost equally well established.

Ireland is also the home of an influential group of Flat-race trainers. Although Irish fortunes, judged by the most exacting international standards, have been at a low ebb for much of the past decade, the characteristic skills and expert horsemanship in Ireland will ensure that the wheel of Turf fortune turns full circle so that once again Irish-trained horses can figure prominently in world racing. Here, then, are three men who can make that happen.

Vincent O'Brien, the Master of Ballydoyle is Ireland's greatest trainer and, arguably, among the most outstanding practitioners of his craft anywhere in the world. O'Brien, whose father farmed and trained in a small way in Co. Cork, began his brilliant and supremely successful career as a jumping trainer, landing a series of

Above left: Nigel Tinkler supervises a Malton gallop.
Keeping going – the all-weather track in use at Jack
Berry's Lancashire stable (left). This early-spring picture
shows a trio of juveniles learning the ropes.

triumphs in such celebrated events as the Grand National, the Cheltenham Gold Cup and the Champion Hurdle. In fact, O'Brien so dominated National Hunt racing in the 1950s that it was inevitable that he would turn his attentions to Flat racing. He acquired the Ballydoyle estate in the Golden Valley country of Co. Tipperary, built spacious boxes and barns and developed a magnificent complex of gallops, all largely financed by his victories in England and astute gambling.

Amazingly, O'Brien's level of achievement in this new discipline not only continued but actually increased. He has won almost every major race throughout Europe including no fewer than six Derbys at Epsom, three Arc de Triomphes and an unparalleled string of Irish, English and French Classic races. His great horses have been legion, but it is impossible to exclude Nijinsky and Alleged from any brief survey of Thoroughbred immortals.

Right: Ireland's top trainer-jockey combination of Dermot Weld and Michael Kinane pictured on the Curragh.

Below: Tommy Stack keeps a careful eye open as his County Tipperary string circle the indoor school.

Now in his seventies and less active on the international scene, Vincent O'Brien remains the greatest trainer of his day and a man whose judgement of young horses has rarely, if ever, been equalled.

Dermot Weld, a veterinary surgeon and former distinguished amateur rider who was Irish champion on three occasions, trains at Rosewell House on the Curragh, the grassy plain in Co. Kildare, some 30 miles south of Dublin, that is Ireland's principal racehorse centre. Although Weld keeps a handful of jumpers even today, it is as a trainer of high-grade Flat racers that he has built an international reputation since first taking out a licence in 1972. He has saddled Classic winners in England and Italy in addition

Above left: No, not General Custer's relief column but Irish trainer Jim Bolger's team pausing to pick the grass in County Carlow.

Left: Irish trainer Jim Bolger watches his daughter Una checking blood test samples at Glebe House Stables, Coolcullen.

Below: Starting stalls practice at Tommy Stack's Thomastown Castle Stables with the trainer himself (left) lending a shoulder and his wife Liz waiting to press the release button.

Above: Tommy Stack at work in the lush Tipperary countryside.
Vincent O'Brien (left), the Master of Ballydoyle.
Curragh trainer John Oxx (right) with Eurobird, the Irish St Leger winner.

to his own country, has an enviable record at Royal Ascot and has been in the winners' enclosure at courses from Doncaster and York to Newmarket, Goodwood and Longchamp.

Versatility is the hallmark of Weld's method. He has long trained for the American real estate millionaire Bertram Firestone and many of his top horses have raced in the colours of that owner. He saddled Blue Wind to land the 1981 Anglo-Irish Oaks double for Firestone's wife Diana but perhaps the best horse he has trained for the Virginian-based husband and wife ownership team was Theatrical, a home-bred colt by Nureyev who, after winning in Europe for Weld, was re-imported to the United States and won the Breeders' Cup Turf at Hollywood Park, Los Angeles, in 1987.

Jim Bolger's yard, Glebe House at out-of-the-

way Coolcullen, Co. Carlow, has the distinction of being Ireland's highest Thoroughbred yard above sea level. But neither its altitude nor remoteness has prevented this aesthetic-looking trainer from producing more than his fair share of important winners under both codes. Among his most notable Flat horses have been Condessa, winner of the 1981 Yorkshire Oaks; Park Appeal, who landed the 1984 Cheveley Park Stakes; Park Express whose successes included the Phoenix Park Champion Stakes and the Nassau Stakes at Goodwood in 1986; and Give Thanks, who put Bolger among Classic-winning company with her victory in the 1983 Irish Oaks.

French trainer Francois Boutin (left), the epitome of Gallic urbanity.

Right: French racing's top team, trainer André Fabre and his jockey Cash Asmussen.

Below: The celebrated Head family gather in Longchamp's 'snake-pit' paddock. Christiane (far left) and her father Alec (centre) are both Prix de l'Arc de Triomphe winning trainers, while jockey brother Freddie (far right) has partnered four winners of France's greatest race.

There is no more immediate or comprehensive statement to make about one's enthusiasm for horseracing than to become an owner, to enjoy the glamour of one's chosen coloured silks being carried to victory. Ask the 10,000 owners registered with the Jockey Club why this holds such a powerful appeal, and the likelihood is that you would receive a similar number of different answers.

Owners are drawn from most of the multi-layered strata of our society: from counts to clergymen, from millionaires to miners. Some own hundreds of horses, others a hundredth of one horse, but give them the opportunity, and they will take a minute or an hour of your time to explain their passion.

Not for nothing is racing called the Sport of Kings. When the first races were run only the richest of the nobility could afford to take part. Today, if you are stricken by a sudden desire to join the ranks of owners, look hard at your bank balance; to keep a horse in training costs £1,000 a month.

To read a trainer's monthly bill is to appreciate a creative work of art. The basic fee is merely the principal item, but is accompanied by authoritative requests for veterinary services, vaccines, shoeing, special feed supplements, gallop fees, and a host of minor items. Some trainers charge for travelling to the races, so you will be making a contribution to that metallic-gold Mercedes which graces the stable entrance. Then there are entry fees, special supplementary fees, early closing prestige races, which are particularly expensive (a runner in the 1989 Ever Ready Derby would go to post having cost his owner £3,000 to take part) and jockeys' fees, together with the costs of transporting the horse to the racecourse; all these have to be taken into account. The basic fee varies between £200 a week or more at one of the top trainers in Newmarket to just under half that in the yard of a small trainer trying to attract owners. Do not begin the drive to the summit unless there is plenty of petrol in the tank!

Flat racing has benefited over more than a quarter of a century from the patronage of **the Queen**, who owned a handful of horses before the death of King George VI in 1952. The best horse to carry the Royal colours for Her Majesty was among the first, a flashy chestnut called Aureole. When Aureole contested the 1953 Derby, the Coronation had been held only a few weeks earlier and the nation's loyalties were divided. Gordon Richards, the most famous jockey in the years after the war, had never ridden the winner of the Derby and took the mount on Pinza, while Harry Carr partnered Aureole, trained by Captain Cecil Boyd-Rochfort. They finished first and second, Pinza galloping away from his white-faced rival to win easily, and as the young Queen congratulated the winning jockey, later to be knighted by her, she must have viewed the outcome of the Classic with mixed emotions.

A fractious individual, Aureole sweated up profusely before the St Leger and could finish only fourth to Premonition, but in 1954 he gave the Queen one of her most memorable days on a racecourse when winning the King George VI and Queen Elizabeth Stakes, leading two fur-

Previous page: One of racing's happiest moments. Her Majesty The Queen greets the 1979 Queen's Vase winner Buttress (Willie Carson). Also pictured (from left) are Lord Porchester, now the Earl of Carnarvon, Michael Oswald, manager of the Royal Stud, Her Majesty the Queen Mother and trainer Dick Hern. And the Royal Ascot sun remembered to shine.

A striking portrait of leading owner Prince Khalid Abdullah (above right).

Maktoum Al-Maktoum (right), eldest of the enthusiastic racing brothers from Dubai.

HH Prince Yazid Saud (left) who has raced horses in this country for the last twelve years.

longs out and holding off the French challenger Vamos by three-quarters of a length. Her Majesty was the leading owner of the season, winning just over £40,000.

Almeria was a top filly in 1957, winning the Ribblesdale Stakes and the Yorkshire Oaks, while Carrozza, leased from the National Stud, carried the Royal colours to victory in the Oaks at Epsom, getting home in a desperate finish thanks to the skills of a young Lester Piggott. Doutelle was another high-class horse who helped to make that season a memorable one.

Carrozza was the first Classic winner to carry the Queen's colours and Her Majesty did not have to wait long for a second. In 1958, despite being considered a second string to the stable's Bold Eagle, Pall Mall and Doug Smith registered a Royal victory in the 2,000 Guineas. However, the season had its disappointments, Almeria and Doutelle chasing home Ballymoss in the King George VI and Queen Elizabeth Stakes.

The first half of the 1960s brought a temporary lull in the Royal fortunes, relieved by the success of Canisbay as a four-year-old in 1965. Ridden by Stan Clayton, the colt just got the better of Roan Rocket for the Eclipse Stakes.

During the next few years, top horses occasionally relieved another dull period for the Royal studs; Magna Carta, Hopeful Venture, Charlton Albany and Example were among the best, trained by Major Hern, Noel Murless and Ian Balding, with Lord Porchester (now Lord Carnarvon) managing the Royal team. The highlights of the first half of the 1970s were the tri-

Right: Willie Carson jumping for joy after landing the 1989 Derby on Nashwan. Owner Hamdan Al-Maktoum is at the dual Classic hero's head.

Below left: The genial, bearded Prince Kais Al-Said, of the ruling family of Oman, celebrates a winner in company with trainer Neville Callaghan (in the raincoat), racing manager Tim Bulwer-Long and jockey Willie Carson.

Below: An excited party surrounds Sheikh Mohammed, in his shirt sleeves, at Newmarket's July meeting in 1986 when members of the Al-Maktoum family owned four of the six winners.

umphs of Highclere, trained by Hern and ridden by Joe Mercer, in the 1,000 Guineas and the Prix de Diane (French Oaks).

The second half of the decade was illuminated by the exploits of Dunfermline, in the Silver Jubilee Year of 1977. Winner of the Oaks, she went to Doncaster to tackle the odds-on Alleged in the St Leger, and in one of the most memorable races for that Classic, beat the O'Brien star (his only defeat) in a stirring finish. The Queen was the leading English breeder of the season.

Yet these heady successes have not been matched more than a decade later. All studs seem to have cyclical fortunes and Her Majesty's have waned a little. Height of Fashion was a high-class two-year-old filly, unbeaten in three races in 1981, and the following season she won the Princess of Wales's Stakes at Newmarket. Sold to Hamdan Al-Maktoum for a price in the region of £1.5 million, Height of Fashion subsequently produced Unfuwain and Nashwan, making even that price something of a bargain.

Soon afterwards it was announced that Her Majesty had bought West Ilsley Stables from the Sobell family, where Dick Hern continued to train, but in the summer of 1988 Hern was asked to retire. Rumours and speculation swept racing throughout the spring of 1989, until eventually a statement was issued which said that Major Hern would be sharing training facilities with William Hastings-Bass, a young trainer from Newmarket who had already prepared several winners for the Queen, including Unknown Quantity, who took the Grade I Arlington Handicap in Chicago in August 1989, the Queen's first winner in America and her first Group winner since Height of Fashion seven years earlier. The Queen will continue to breed and race quality animals, and one day may hit the jackpot with a Derby winner. Imagine the scenes on Epsom Downs that day!

The victory of Hatta in the Molecomb Stakes at Goodwood in 1977 went almost unremarked. John Dunlop had sent out a nice two-year-old filly to win a Group race for a young Arab by the name of Sheikh Mohammed. No one anticipated that, a dozen years on, the **Maktoum family** of Dubai would be the single most powerful force in the world of the Thoroughbred.

Two years later **Sheikh Mohammed** swept into the Keeneland July sales with his principal adviser of that day, Colonel Dick Warden, and began to do battle with the Robert Sangster

team. There followed the years of madness when bloodstock prices soared on a tidal wave of oil money, driven sky high by the Arab sheikhs of the Middle East. In less than a decade the Maktoum family, rulers of Dubai, one of the Emirates on the southern coast of the Persian Gulf, has built up a power base which has brought many of the world's top Thoroughbreds

Lord Howard de Walden doffs his top hat to lead in the 1985 Derby winner Slip Anchor (Steve Cauthen), while trainer Henry Cecil's face, peeping over the nose of a police horse (right), shows the emotion of racing's greatest day.

to race in Britain. The empire has developed on an unprecedented scale, and is still growing.

Sheikh Raschid bin Saeed Al-Maktoum is the ruler of Dubai, and he has four sons. The eldest, Sheikh Maktoum, is the Crown Prince of the Emirate, followed by Sheikh Hamdan, Sheikh Mohammed and Sheikh Ahmed. While Sheikh Mohammed was and is the driving force behind this huge investment, his brothers have become more and more captivated by the sport, and consequently take a closer interest in the horses which carry their own colours.

Their influence is not confined to the United Kingdom. The family has top-class horses in France, Australia and America, although most of those who race in the United States have initially

Above: Prince Khalid Abdullah receives the Swettenham Stud Sussex Stakes trophy from Robert Sangster following the victory of his colt Rousillon at Goodwood in 1985.

Above right: HH the Aga Khan proudly leads his 1986 Derby winner Shahrastani and a smiling Walter Swinburn towards the unsaddling enclosure.

Right: The Princess of Wales's Stakes at Newmarket in 1982 with Willie Carson driving Height of Fashion home to win in the Royal colours. The Queen subsequently sold her filly to Hamdan Al-Maktoum and she bred him Derby winner Nashwan, Unfuwain and Mukddaam.

been trained in England and, at each annual assessment, have been deemed more suited for a career on the other side of the Atlantic.

In addition to bloodstock, they have bought and refurbished a dozen studs to the highest standards, and they have made many significant contributions to the sport, including the *Racing Post* newspaper, the Al Bahathri all-weather gallop at Newmarket and a dozen important race sponsorships. The eagle eye of the taxman put an end to the cash bonanza which brightened the lives of their staff in the early days, but those who work for the Maktoums have no complaints.

The men from Dubai have been greeted with near-universal acclaim, with only a few dissenting voices. Occasionally their champions are kept apart in order to preserve their reputations; the ordinary English punter finds it hard to pronounce, let alone recognize, many of the esoteric Arabic names which their horses carry; and smaller trainers get frustrated by running their

108

modest animals against million-dollar blue-bloods in little maiden races. But the overall impact has been highly beneficial.

Sheikh Mohammed has the most horses in training of the family and his Darley Stud Management empire also encompasses the horses owned by the youngest brother, Ahmed. The studs are managed in England and America by Robert Acton, and in Ireland by Michael Osborne, while Anthony Stroud is racing manager for the operation.

Educated in England and a competent pilot, Sheikh Mohammed's action-man image is one he enjoys. At home he is entertained by the exploits of his hawks, his camels, and recently by horses running on a newly-constructed racecourse.

An excellent judge of a horse, Sheikh Mohammed accompanies the entourage of managers, vets and pedigree experts when they descend on the bloodstock sales, and often makes the final decisions. He rides out with his trainers when visiting Newmarket, and, if the demands on his time in Dubai were not so compelling, he would like nothing better than to train horses. The centre of the operation is at Dalham Hall Stud, Newmarket, bought in 1981. Here some of the world's finest young stallions, either owned wholly or in part by Sheikh Mohammed, stand (see 'Sources of Horses').

Oh So Sharp, Diminuendo, Pebbles and Sonic Lady have been the best fillies to carry Sheikh

Below: Lavinia, Duchess of Norfolk (centre) in good humour after seeing her colt Sheriff's Star win at Ascot. Her trainer-daughter Lady Herries joins in the joke with bloodstock advisor Peter Willett (right) and Rodney Masters, chief racing reporter of the Press Association.

Below right: Lady Beaverbrook joins in the applause for Willie Carson after he had ridden her colt Minster Son to victory in the 1988 St Leger. The popular Scottish jockey also bred this Doncaster Classic hero.

Mohammed's colours, while Sure Blade, Ajdal, Soviet Star, Polish Precedent and Old Vic have been the most successful colts. In between there have been scores of Group race winners and if Sheikh Mohammed has not yet won the Derby or the Arc de Triomphe, it is only a matter of time before those glittering prizes come his way.

Among his many responsibilities at home, Sheikh Mohammed is the Minister of Defence, while **Sheikh Ahmed** is the Commander-in-Chief of the Army. Sheikh Ahmed's best horse by a mile was Mtoto, dual winner of the Eclipse Stakes and an unlucky second in the Prix de l'Arc de Triomphe after winning the King George VI and Queen Elizabeth Diamond Stakes as a four-year-old.

Similarly **Sheikh Hamdan** is mainly associated with Nashwan who, in 1989, became the first horse to win the 2,000 Guineas, Derby, Eclipse and King George in a season. Sheikh Hamdan's principal stud is the home for

Nashwan and that champion's half-brother, Unfuwain. In the autumn of 1989 Sheikh Hamdan bought Farncombe Down, in Berkshire, to be built as a new stable in which Dick Hern will train from 1991, a gesture which was welcomed by the whole racing community.

The colours of **Maktoum Al-Maktoum**, whose bloodstock interests are managed by Michael Goodbody at the Gainsborough Stud, were carried to victory by Shareef Dancer in the Irish Derby. Sheikh Maktoum won the St Leger with Touching Wood, the 2,000 Guineas with Shadeed, and the 1,000 Guineas with Ma Biche, bought during the winter prior to her three-year-old career. Quality as well as quantity is the hallmark of the Maktoum empire.

Nor are they the only Arabs to have made a mark. The quiet, polite Saudi Arabian **Prince Khalid Abdullah** does not race on the same scale, but his operation, based at Juddmonte Farm Stud, Berkshire, has produced some top-

Right: Stavros Niarchos receives the magnificent trophy from Lady March after his horse Valuable Witness had won the 1985 Goodwood Cup.

Sir Michael Sobell (right) and his son-in-law Lord Weinstock with the trophy won by Troy in the 200th running of the Derby.

The distinguished American racehorse owner and philanthropist Paul Mellon (extreme right), owner-breeder of the 1971 Derby and Prix de l'Arc de Triomphe winner Mill Reef.

Louis and Valerie Freedman (below), photographed at their Cliveden Stud in Berkshire.

Below right: The great mare Triptych after winning the 1988 Hanson Coronation Cup at Epsom for the second successive year.

class racehorses in recent years, including Known Fact, Rainbow Quest and Warning.

Khalid Abdullah retains Pat Eddery, the jockey who rode the mighty Dancing Brave to victories for the Prince in the King George and Prix de l'Arc de Triomphe, while that horse's successes in the 2,000 Guineas and the Eclipse were gained under Greville Starkey.

The Juddmonte Farm umbrella includes three studs in England, one in Ireland and one in America. The horses are trained by Guy Harwood and, until the end of 1989, Jeremy Tree. Prince Khalid has been one of the most successful owners of recent times, and with his emphasis on quality will surely remain so for years to come.

For a decade, **Robert Sangster** ruled the world of European racing. He was born into wealth, his father owning Vernons Football Pools, and he began his interest in racing with some modest purchases, trained by Eric Cousins, near Sangster's Swettenham Stud in Cheshire. Many of the early winners carried the colours of his first wife, but in the early 1970s Sangster decided to turn the ownership of Thoroughbred

racehorses from a hobby into a commodity. His policy was to employ the best and when Vincent O'Brien and Lester Piggott were chosen as his trainer and jockey, no one in Europe questioned his judgement.

Concentrating on purchasing the best stock available from Northern Dancer, the legendary American stallion, Sangster employed a team of pedigree experts, horsemen and vets to sift the yearlings available at the top bloodstock sales on both sides of the Atlantic. He was prepared to take on anyone, and the first significant rewards came in 1977, when The Minstrel won the Derby and the King George VI and Queen Elizabeth II Diamond Stakes. In that same year another colt, Alleged, improved dramatically throughout the second half of the season and carried the green and blue Sangster colours to victory in the Prix de l'Arc de Triomphe, a feat the colt was able to repeat the following year.

The big winners seemed to flow in an incessant stream. By now Sangster had 70 mares in Europe, half that number in Australia, and owned part of 30 horses in Vincent O'Brien's stable as well as others in America and Down

Under. He owned studs in England, Ireland and France.

By the end of the 1970s the love affair between Piggott and the Sangster–O'Brien combination was on the wane. No fully documented explanation exists, but Piggott, reaching the twilight of his career, certainly found the travelling to and from Ireland irksome. Piggott joined Henry Cecil at Warren Place, renewing his partnership with several owners, while Pat Eddery was awarded the job at Ballydoyle. After landing the 1982 Derby with Golden Fleece, two years later O'Brien sent out El Gran Señor to win the 2,000 Guineas but, given a controversial ride by Eddery in the Derby, Sangster's colt was narrowly beaten by Secreto, trained by O'Brien's son, David.

Sangster, O'Brien and John Magnier have built up one of the most important studs in Europe at Coolmore but Sangster, who had made a multi-million pound investment in Manton, now one of the country's most prestigious training centres, offered the Wiltshire Compex for sale again in 1989. Sangster employed Michael Dickinson to set up Manton. The young Yorkshireman had established himself as a National Hunt maestro, but before the end of this first season of full operation, Dickinson and Sangster parted company. Intense, dedicated and innovative, Dickinson never quite shared Sangster's relaxed style, and Manton is now run by Barry Hills, who formerly had sent out many runners in the Sangster colours from his Lambourn yard.

A bon viveur, Sangster may no longer be the leading force in Europe, but his team continues to make shrewd purchases at the sales with an eye to reasonable value for money. Coolmore has some fine stallions and although many are prepared to bet that Sangster's supremacy is over, few believe that we have seen the last of him in the Classic winner's enclosure.

When the present **Aga Khan** inherited his father's bloodstock interests in 1960, he wasn't sure he wanted to continue to maintain one of the most powerful equine empires in Europe. However, the Harvard graduate decided that, provided it could be run as a cost-effective operation, it would provide employment in the area around his estate and he undertook the challenge.

He sent Blushing Groom, third in The Minstrel's Derby and one of the best of his generation, to America and used the funds to finance the purchase of the Marcel Boussac and Madame

Dupre stock at knockdown prices. In 1978 he decided to dispatch some of his team to be trained in England, by Michael Stoute, Fulke Johnson Houghton, and, nowadays, Luca Cumani. He has approaching 200 horses in training each season, divided between England, Ireland and France.

As an owner and breeder the Aga Khan has enjoyed considerable success, but occasionally has become involved in controversy. After Vayraan had won the 1981 Champion Stakes a subsequent dope test found traces of steroids, although exhaustive research demonstrated beyond doubt that the horse had produced the substance naturally. Lashkari and Shernazar were disqualified in America for failing dope tests, only to be reinstated, and the Aga Khan owned Shergar, one of the best winners of the Derby, who was kidnapped and killed, presumably as an IRA plot to blackmail the owners.

Aliysa won the Oaks for the Aga Khan in 1989, but a post-race test identified a prohibited substance. At the time of writing, Jockey Club enquiries were continuing. Suffice to say that the Aga Khan, the Imam of the Ismailis and 51st in direct line from the Prophet Mohammed, has a reputation for honesty second to none.

The Aga Khan does not raid bloodstock sales. He breeds his own racehorses, and, in addition to the mighty Shergar, his luxurious racing complex at Aiglemont, Chantilly, has been responsible for the likes of Shahrastani, Natroun, Kahyasi and Doyoun. To have won the Derby three times in a decade is an achievement some of his big-spending rivals may never match.

One stalwart of British racing for a quarter of a century has been **Lady Beaverbrook**, who inherited a fortune when her husband died in 1964. Together with the late David Robinson, a reclusive millionaire who lived in Cambridge, and Indian shipping tycoon Ravi Tikkoo, she was among the biggest spenders of the era at the yearling sales. Her first Classic success came with Bustino in the 1974 St Leger, at a time when she had spent some £3 million on bloodstock, a fortune before the era of Robert Sangster and the Arabs. Bustino was a high-class three-year-old who failed behind Snow Knight in the Derby, but gave a hint of what was to come when landing the Great Voltigeur Stakes at York in August and Lady Beaverbrook's perseverance was rewarded at Doncaster the following month.

Winner of the Coronation Cup in record time the following year, Bustino will be best remembered for his narrow defeat by Grundy in the King George VI and Queen Elizabeth Stakes of 1975, one of the very few battles to merit that overworked description 'Race of the Century'.

At one stage the most intractable of colts,

Gymcrack Racing management team of (left to right) Peter Easterby, his son Tim and Gordon Holmes, at work in the Great Habton office.

Above: Luca Cumani and a group of owners watching work on the Warren Hill gallop at Newmarket.

Jim Joel (right), the Grand Old Man of British racing, greeting High Estate in the winners' enclosure at Sandown Park.

Boldboy was transformed by being gelded into one of the sport's toughest, most reliable racehorses and won a clutch of Group races over sprint distances, including the Vernons Sprint Cup and the Abernant Stakes three times. Relkino won the Benson & Hedges Gold Cup for Lady Beaverbrook in 1976 and the Lockinge Stakes the following year, while Niniski came close to giving her a second St Leger victory finishing behind Son of Love and Soleil Noir in 1979.

While Lady Beaverbrook might not have had as many horses in training during the past few seasons as earlier, her 'beaver brown and maple green' colours have continued to enjoy considerable success and one of the highlights of her involvement came in 1985 with Petoski. Unplaced to Slip Anchor in the Derby, Petoski gave a glimpse of what was to come when taking the Princess of Wales's Stakes at the Newmarket July Meeting and later in the year avenged the defeat of Bustino in the King George VI and Queen Elizabeth Diamond Stakes by defeating Oh So Sharp in a dramatic finish. Given a

tremendous ovation by the crowd in the unsaddling enclosure, a mark of respect and thanks for her contribution, Lady Beaverbrook told the Press that Petoski's success coincided with her 75th birthday.

Her horses are rarely precocious; they are mostly bred to stay a mile and a half, but the Derby has so far eluded Lady Beaverbrook. However, she came closest when Terimon chased home Nashwan in 1989, and the previous year gained another Classic success when Minster Son galloped to victory in the St Leger, being both bred and ridden by Willie Carson.

Lady Beaverbrook believes number 7 to be lucky, and the names of her horses (unless named at the time of purchase) carry seven letters, a foible which appears to have brought her

considerable success on the racecourse. She appears rarely, but if there is one owner the public would like to win the Derby, other than the Queen, it would be Marcia, Lady Beaverbrook.

Another major supporter of English racing has been **Paul Mellon**, an American multi-millionaire. When his father learned of his son's interest in racing, he observed: 'Every fool knows that one horse can run faster than another', but it didn't dim Mellon's fascination with the game. He owns Rokeby Farm in the United States, which has consistently produced high-class racehorses, but Mellon will always be associated in this country with Mill Reef.

The owner of the most valuable private collection of sporting art in the world, Mellon bred the mighty Mill Reef at Rokeby. Ian Balding at Kingsclere trained the handsome little colt to become the champion of his day, meeting defeat as a three-year-old only at the hands of Brigadier Gerard in the 2,000 Guineas, over a distance which was short of Mill Reef's best. The Derby, Eclipse, King George and Arc de Triomphe all came within Mill Reef's compass.

An honorary member of the Jockey Club, Mellon donated Mill Reef to the National Stud when his Derby and Arc de Triomphe winner had recovered from the fractured leg which ended the colt's career, a lasting legacy to the sport.

Lord Howard de Walden is an owner-breeder of an old-fashioned type now all but eliminated by successsive estate duties. His Plantation and Thornton Studs have consistently produced successful horses for a generation. Kris was the top miler of his day, but the principal reward for a lifetime's devotion to the sport, which included two terms as Senior Steward of the Jockey Club, came in 1985 when Slip Anchor stormed away with the Derby.

Louis Freedman, a former deputy Senior Steward of the Jockey Club, has enjoyed two decades of success as an owner-breeder, sending his mares from Cliveden Stud to the best stallions, and the produce to the best trainers. Polygamy won the Oaks in his yellow and black colours, but he realized his cherished ambition when Reference Point won the Derby of 1987, followed by the King George and the St Leger. A cheer went up when Reference Point flashed across the line at Epsom, a home-bred winner owned by an Englishman!

The black and white silks of **Charles St George**, closely associated with Lester Piggott, have been part of English racing for 30 years, and while the Derby has eluded St George, whose horses are trained at Sefton Lodge by Henry Cecil, he has won an Oaks with Ginevra and two St Legers with Bruni and Michelozzo.

Although Ardross narrowly failed in the Arc, he won a clutch of Cup races, and is now a stallion in demand.

Lord Howard de Walden owns acres of central London and is one of the wealthiest men in the country, while Louis Freedman is a banker. For those without such resources, owning a stud is prohibitively expensive. Most owners have one or two horses, bought at yearling sales, but the Jocky Club does permit partnerships of up to 12 in any horse, a form of syndication which has drawn many new enthusiasts into the ranks of owners.

In the past few years, more widely available opportunities have been made to suit different pockets. Vincent O'Brien and partners launched **Classic Thoroughbreds** on the Dublin Stock Exchange, a company formed to buy high-class yearlings and race them, with a view to finding the champions which would make stallions. So far the stock, in both senses, has not met with expectations, but one champion could change all that.

The British Thoroughbred Racing and Breeding Company owns racehorses and breeds from its own mares for the benefit of its many members, but has to rely heavily on revenue from its own premium-rate telephone service information lines to balance the books. The organization is based at Fyfield House, which was bought from trainer Toby Balding, who is a leading light in the company.

Full Circle is the brainchild of Colin Tinkler. The company, formed specifically to race horses, charges £450 per share, which lasts for a year, when the stock is sold. Members usually receive about £50 in return. Full Circle lost £800,000 in its most recent year, but Tinkler's thousands of members are more than delighted with the performance of the company, which enables them to stand (a few at a time!) cheek by jowl with Royalty, foreign princes, oil millionaires, shipping magnates and property tycoons in the parade ring.

Several more companies have been launched in the wake of Full Circle and BTRB, some with only a brief life, and prospective customers are urged to read the small print with a powerful pair of binoculars before signing up. All owners must be registered with the Jockey Club, which sends out a questionnaire to aspirants. Under the heading 'profession' the form states: 'the term gentleman will not suffice'. Not so long ago, it would have been the sole criterion.

Racegoers' Club President Tony Fairbairn and Secretary Louise Gold pictured racing at Ascot. The Club, established more than twenty five years ago, pioneered public ownership of horses.

JOCKEYS

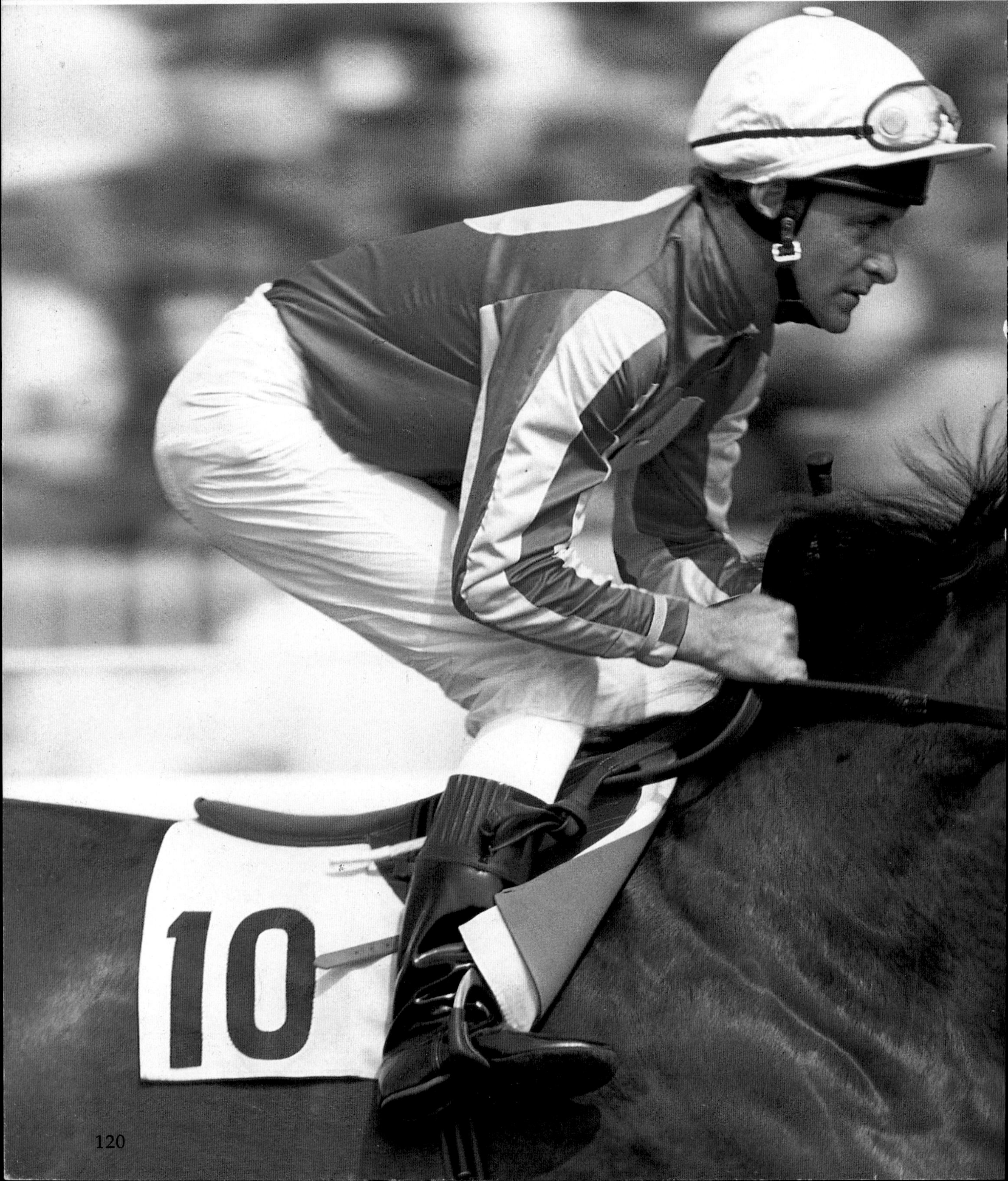

The art of jockeyship is not, by any means, always synonymous with the broader requirements of horsemanship. Some professional race riders might be described as horsemen first and jockeys second but more than a few of racing's greatest international superstars learned their skills by a form of equestrian shorthand rather than by the painstaking methods resulting from more formal teaching. In fact, in an age when the vast majority of people in this country neither ride nor have any great desire to do so, many trainers prefer to take on raw recruits as would-be apprentices rather than employ half-taught youngsters who may have already picked up bad habits which are nearly impossible to eradicate.

It is, of course, possible to learn the basic requirements of riding comparatively quickly but the finer points of jockeyship—the ability to make a horse quicken, for instance, or the proper application of the whip and its switching from one hand to another without causing a horse to become unbalanced or lose momentum—are precise refinements which only constant practice can provide, even for the most naturally gifted.

The social history of British horseracing has seen a greater change in the status of professional jockeys than in any other element of the Turf community. During the 19th century all but a handful of the most outstanding and successful

Champions of a quarter century ago (above). The great Australian jockey Scobie Breasley leads his legendary rival Lester Piggott.

Francis (Frank) Buckle (above right), the greatest jockey of his day and rider of 27 Classic winners in a remarkable career which spanned 50 years.

Top right: The Alfred Munnings portrait of Sir Gordon Richards on Sun Chariot which hangs in the National Horseracing Museum at Newmarket.

All our yesterdays . . . trainer Geoff Lewis (above right, centre), a pound or two heavier than in his regular riding days, kitted out for the Manton Plate which he won.

Former champion jockey Joe Mercer (above centre, extreme right) towards the end of his outstanding career in the saddle.

Right: The Manton Plate for retired jockeys. Epsom trainer Geoff Lewis (far side) leads from the start.

Previous page: A master of his craft, seven-times champion Pat Eddery.

riders were looked upon as nothing more than poorly-paid servants. Many of the early racing records omitted the name of the winning rider and where such facts were recorded only the jockey's surname appears.

What a transformation now! In modern times, top riders, like the stars of the golfing world or the international tennis circuit, are millionaires, feted and fawned over with all the attendant showbusiness glamour. In many instances they are more wealthy than the owners and trainers

Gordon Richards on 'Sun Chariot'.

who employ them, but in respect to racing tradition they still assume a posture of subservience to them. But a present-day jockey, richly rewarded though he is, leads an exhausting life with the heavy demands of international travel frequently combined with a near-starvation diet in order to maintain a maximum riding weight sometimes as much as two stones under natural level.

The need to diet is not a modern phenomenon. **Fred Archer** (1857–86), one of the greatest race riders, suffered the pangs of acute hunger throughout his all-too-short career and it was unquestionably the need for constant 'wasting' which contributed to the depression which led to his suicide at the age of 29. Archer set new standards of professional competence which, combined with his natural intelligence and assertive personality, led to phenomenal professional success. His will to win was singular and perhaps best illustrated by the—probably apocryphal—story that he once burst into tears because he could not ride both winners in a dead-heat! Although ruthless in his ambition and a rough rider when occasion demanded, Archer also had considerable charm. Like Lester Piggott, with whom his career is so often compared, Archer's ultra-careful approach to financial matters meant that he left upwards of £60,000, a huge sum in 1886.

Born near Cheltenham and the son of a jump jockey, he was apprenticed at the age of 11 to the fashionable Newmarket trainer Mathew Dawson at Heath House in 1868, and rode his first winner two years later. At the time of his tragic death his professional career spanned just 17 years but during that time he was champion jockey on no fewer than 13 occasions and partnered 2,748 winners, 21 of them in Classic races, landing the Derby five times and six St Legers. Archer was the *enfant terrible* of 19th century racing, a young man of precocious talent and exceptional skill but he was not the first of the Turf's great jockeys.

Pride of place in any attempt to name in sequence such a list of racing stars must surely go to **Frank Buckle** (1766–1832) who rode 27

Yves Saint-Martin (above left), France's greatest jockey and fifteen-times winner of the Cravache d'Or.

Lester Piggott (above right), arguably the greatest jockey in international racing history.

Left: Lester Piggott towers above his American friend and rival Bill Shoemaker. Their aggregate total of world-wide winners topped 14,000.

Right: Ormonde, the 1886 Derby winner with Fred Archer in the saddle and trainer John Porter at the great colt's head. Note Archer's length of irons.

Classic winners, a record which remained unsurpassed until 1984 when the peerless Piggott rode Commanche Run to victory in the St Leger to topple Buckle's name from the top of the list. Unlike Archer and, indeed, Piggott, Buckle never suffered a weight problem. Born in Newmarket, the son of a saddler, he was tiny as a boy—tipping the scales at under 4 stones when riding in public for the first time in 1783. Nearly half a century later, when riding for the last time at the age of 65, he still weighed in at only 7 stone 11 pounds.

Although always careful with his diet, he never needed to waste and would occasionally treat himself to a roast goose for dinner. Supremely fit, Buckle lived for many years on a farm near Peterborough where he raised fatstock and bred greyhounds, fighting cocks and bulldogs, making an almost daily 92-mile round trip to Newmarket on one of his hacks in order to race and ride gallops. He must have been a familiar and respected figure on the Fenland highroads on his immaculate mounts with his tiny figure wrapped in a voluminous white cape.

Francis Buckle was unquestionably the greatest jockey of his day and lived well on the

Former French champion jockey Freddie Head (top left), four times winner of the Prix de l'Arc de Triomphe.

Smiling in the rain, Irish jockey Christy Roche (above, extreme left).

The much-travelled Irish jockey Declan Gillespie (above left).

Striding out in great style, Ray Cochrane (left) seeks to lose overweight.

Paul Eddery (below left), looking slightly surprised to be 'in shot'.

Greville Starkey (below right), who retired at the end of the 1989 season with more than 2,000 winners to his credit.

Right: Walter Swinburn making the best possible use of his time – checking the form of the runners while taking off a pound or two in the sauna at his Newmarket home.

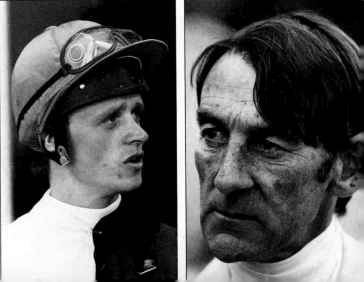

proceeds. Racing was his life and when he finally decided to retire from the saddle he lived only a few months more.

William Scott (1797–1848), a contemporary of Buckle's, was also a Newmarket man but did most of his race riding in the north, his brother John having an outstandingly successful stable at Malton in Yorkshire from which he sent out no fewer than 40 Classic winners, including a record 16 scorers in the St Leger. Bill Scott himself rode the winners of 19 Classics but his career would have been of even greater significance had he not been a dishonest, gambling drunkard with a coarse and aggressive manner.

Six of his nine St Leger victories came on horses saddled by his brother as did the Derby triumphs on Atilla (1842) and Cotherstone the following year. Bill Scott won both the 2,000 Guineas and St Leger of 1846 on a colt named Sir Tatton Sykes, which he also owned; but the horse missed out on the distinction of completing that year's Triple Crown when beaten just a neck in the Derby under an abysmal ride from Scott, who was palpably drunk.

James 'Jem' Robinson (1793–1865) was another top Newmarket jockey of the same era and Scott's great rival, the two men clearly having mutual feelings of considerable animosity. Robinson rode more winners of the Derby (six) than any jockey until Lester Piggott and achieved a total of 24 Classic victories. This son of a farm labourer was apprenticed to Robert Robson at a time when Frank Buckle was senior jockey to the same Newmarket stable and it was from Buckle that Robinson acquired many of his race-riding skills, a fact he freely acknowledged towards the end of his life.

Robinson, considered to be a man to whom sportsmanship and honesty were second nature, unfortunately had a character defect—he was impulsively generous and fond of high living. He liked nothing better than to take rooms in London during the closed season and indulge himself in every type of extravagance, with the result that he spent the last few years of his life in abject poverty alleviated only by the charity of friends.

Gordon Richards (1904–86) achieved a degree of social standing no professional jockey before or since could match. The first member of his craft to receive the accolade of knighthood, the Shropshire miner's son—one of twelve children—was also the first jockey to be elected an honorary member of the misnamed Jockey

Left: The Royal jockey, Mr William Hunter Carson, OBE.

Below: Pat Eddery pictured with his mentor, the late 'Frenchie' Nicholson. In the background stands another celebrated trainer, Freddie Maxwell.

Bottom: Oh, brother! Twins Richard (far side) and Michael Hills fight out the finish of Epsom's Blue Riband Trial. Richard's mount Shuja won this 1988 clash in a photo finish from St Cadoc, trained by the boys' father Barry Hills.

Right: A Papal blessing from 11-times South African champion Michael Roberts, as he returns in triumph on Mtoto after winning the 1988 Coral-Eclipse Stakes at Sandown.

Below: Kahyasi, the 1988 Derby winner, going to post for the Lingfield Trial under Ray Cochrane.

Stylish Steve Cauthen (bottom), a champion on both sides of the Atlantic.

129

Club, two distinctions which remain unique to this day. Richards was a folk hero and throughout his peak years thousands of day-to-day backers would follow his mounts with blind devotion because of the well-founded conviction that 'Gordon always tries'.

During the period 1920 to 1954 Sir Gordon Richards rode 4,870 winners in Britain and was champion jockey a record 26 times. It is, therefore, a curious statistic that he partnered a mere 14 Classic winning mounts. It is not intended to reflect anything but praise to write of Richards that he was the greatest bread-and-butter jockey of them all, but that he might have lacked the cool head to succeed on the great occasions of racing in quite the same way as his younger contemporary, Lester Piggott.

Richards did not enjoy immediate success when he began as an apprentice with Martin Hartigan at Foxhill in Wiltshire. His first victory, in a boys' race at Leicester in 1921, was followed by only four more that season and in 1922 he could not better that figure. But the next two years saw him partner 49 and 61 winners and his great career in the saddle was properly underway. The young Richards suddenly and spectacularly blossomed in his first season after coming out of his indentureship, landing the

Left: Tony Clark returning to unsaddle on Juddmonte International winner Ile de Chypre at York. This Group I success was the biggest of Clark's career to date.

Right: Well done, darling! John Reid gets an Arc-winning kiss from his wife Joy following the triumph of Tony Bin at Longchamp, 1988.

Below left: Channel 4 interviewer Derek Thompson seeks the view of French-based star Tony Cruz and his lovely wife.

Below: In the words of W. S. Gilbert, 'I am generally admired'. Steve Cauthen and friends at Royal Ascot, 1989.

first of his championship titles with 118 winners. But early in 1926 he was taken gravely ill with tuberculosis and was obliged to spend some months in a sanatorium.

His determination was such that he regained his leading position in the title race of 1927. From then on his illustrious career was a series of triumphs interrupted only by the outbreak of the Second World War. Of the great races only the Derby—arguably the greatest of them all—continued to elude him and it was not until the Coronation Year of 1953 and just after the new Queen had conferred his knighthood that Sir Gordon, dubbed The Shortest Knight by a memorable contemporary newspaper heading,

Left: Ajdal at full stretch under Walter Swinburn to land the 1987 July Cup.

Veteran Bruce Raymond taking things easy (right).

A rare collection of riding talent leaving the Royal Ascot weighing room (below). Left to right: Cash Asmussen, Pat Eddery, Ray Cochrane, Tony Ives and Michael Roberts.

Jockey Michael Kinane (below right) looks apprehensive at the welcome for his 1989 Arc partner Carroll House.

finally achieved his ultimate professional ambition. In his 28th and final attempt at Epsom glory, he drove Pinza to a four-length victory. It was the supreme irony that Her Majesty's candidate, Aureole, finished second.

Richards had decided to retire at the end of 1954 but at the Eclipse fixture at Sandown Park that summer the filly Abergeldie reared up leaving the paddock for the Star Stakes, leaving her jockey with a fractured pelvis and four dislocated ribs. Sir Gordon never rode in public again but went on to train with considerable success. A fine jockey, his entire life provided proof positive that a true gentleman can spring from the humblest origins.

Doug Smith was champion in 1954 and for four of the next five seasons but by the early 1960s Lester Piggott and the Australian **Scobie Breasley** had become the dominant figures of British jockeyship. Piggott won a total of 11 titles during his extraordinary and often controversial career while Breasley, more than 20 years his senior, was champion on four occasions. Their battles for supremacy provided an abiding subject for discussion and argument among the racing community and punters alike. Their

riding styles were strongly contrasting. Piggott, flamboyant and unconventional but supremely gifted, was a more eye-catching jockey than the quiet and self-effacing little Australian but whatever their respective merits, both men possessed the skill and flair to excite public adulation.

Lester Piggott has fascinated the public since riding his first winner at Haydock Park in 1948. He continues to do so. Enigmatic and anti-authoritarian, he was without doubt one of the greatest jockeys in the international history of horse racing but while the entire racing public gave him admiration and support during his long riding career, they were equally gripped by his curious character. His taut, pale face with that surprisingly charming lop-sided smile has appeared in literally thousands of newspapers, magazines and books; on film and television.

At the pinnacle of his fame he was instantly recognizable to millions, the most famous sportsman in Britain and one of the country's most newsworthy personalities. His gifts as a jockey were unmatched but he was never fully conscious of his own fame and, probably because partial deafness makes communication difficult, certainly never encouraged public participation in his private life. Despite this reluctance, Piggott was constantly in the full glare of publicity.

The few people who can claim to know him well find the man humorous and engaging but to the majority of his fans Piggott is a remote figure. Quite possibly, that very facet of his character, allied to the almost legendary application of his skill and strength in the saddle, has only encouraged unwelcome if unavoidable attention.

Lester Piggott may have been bred to be a jockey but was ill-equipped by nature for the role, growing too tall by normally accepted racing standards. His father, Keith, had been a jockey who became a Grand National-winning trainer but Lester was more the physical stamp of his grandfather, Ernest, a jump rider of great

Top Northern apprentice Alan Munro (top left).

The successful North Country jockey Kevin Darley (above, extreme left).

Ian Johnson (above left), one of the jockeys injured in the Portland Handicap pile-up at Doncaster in September, 1989.

Mark Birch (left), a stalwart of Northern racing.

Opposite page: Dale 'Hairpin' Gibson (above right). Among the best apprentice jockeys in the country and certainly the tallest.

Right: Rambo's Hall and Dean McKeown are led in, covered in mud and glory, after winning the 1989 William Hill Cambridgeshire.

renown with three Grand National victories to
his credit. Lester's mother was born Iris Rickaby,
daughter of Frederick Rickaby who rode three
Classic winners, and sister to Frederick Lester
Rickaby, who rode five before losing his life
serving with the Royal Tank Regiment in France
in 1918 and after whom the young Piggott was
named. One of Frederick Lester Rickaby's sons,
Bill, himself became a celebrated jockey who
won both the 1961 1,000 Guineas and Oaks on
Sweet Solera and the following season's 2,000
Guineas on Privy Councillor.

But Lester Piggott's Turf pedigree goes back a
great deal further: to the mid-1700s, in fact,
when his great-great-great-great grandfather,
John Day, trained on Houghton Downs in
Hampshire. This venerable gentleman was
reputed to have weighed in at well over 20
stones while his son, John Barham Day, tipped
the scales at barely a third of that bulk. John
junior, one of the greatest jockeys of the early
19th century, was responsible for no fewer than
16 Classic winners and subsequently trained a
further 10. His brothers, Samuel, Charles, William and James, all rode with varying degrees of
success. Lester Piggott's own grandfather,
Ernest, married Margeret Cannon, sister of one
champion jockey, Mornington Cannon, and
daughter of another, Thomas Cannon, who was
married to Catherine Day, a great-grand-
daughter of Old John Day, founder of this
remarkable racing dynasty. So, in bloodstock
terms, Lester Piggott was bred 'in the purple'
and his great career provided living proof of that
timeless racing cliché, 'jockeys are born and not
made'.

Lester Piggott's record of achievements
eclipsed even those of his distinguished
forebears, however, chief among them his
record total of 29 Classic successes and his
unmatched total, for an English jockey, of more
than 5,000 career winners. His fabulous riding
career ended just before his 50th birthday and
he switched to training. The transition appeared
to be reasonably painless and he won with his
first runner at Royal Ascot. The racing community awaited with pleasurable anticipation the
news that Piggott would follow the example of
Gordon Richards by being knighted.

No such announcement came from Bucking-
ham Palace. Instead, to the horror of his countless admirers, came news that Piggott had been
arrested at his Newmarket home and charged
with massive tax evasion. In October 1987 he
was sentenced to three years' imprisonment for
attempting to defraud the Inland Revenue and
the VAT department of Customs and Excise of a
total in the region of £1.75 million. He served
only a third of that term before being released on

parole in the autumn of 1988 but lasting damage had been done to the reputation of a great sporting hero.

There is no question that Lester Piggott was the greatest jockey of his era and probably the finest of all time. Those fortunate to see him at the peak of his powers will never forget that unique combination of strength and finesse; of oneness with the horse. Many will find it in their hearts to forgive him a character weakness which the trial judge, Mr Justice Farquharson, was unable to overlook. Lester Piggott may be a fallen idol but to a whole generation of British racing fans he will always remain the 'Long Fellow' of a thousand memories.

Joe Mercer, a fine rider in his own right and both a friend and rival of Piggott's for many years, summed up the feelings of so many when he said: 'Lester is different and you need to make allowances for that. But he was the greatest jockey any of us are ever likely to see and my admiration for his skills cannot be changed by what happened afterwards.'

In strictly race-riding terms, what happened afterwards was the era of Pat Eddery and Steve Cauthen whose battles for the championship were as fiercely contested as those between Lester Piggott and Scobie Breasley of two decades earlier. **Pat Eddery** was born into a racing

Diana Grissell (above left) has her daughter Hanna to help carry the tack at Lingfield Park in 1986.

Thumbs up from Lanfranco Dettori (left), champion apprentice of 1989 and No. 1 jockey to fellow-countryman Luca Cumani's powerful stable for 1990.

Right: An unusual group picture taken at York in 1988, of the Great Britain v. Europe Ladies' International Team Race.

Below: George Duffield – Mr Consistent.

family in Dublin on 18 March 1952. His father, Jimmy Eddery, was a former Irish champion jockey who rode Panaslipper to victory in the Irish Derby and landed the Irish Oaks on Silken Glider. Pat's mother was the daughter of steeplechase jockey Jack Moylan who rode Fly Mask into second place in the 1924 Grand National.

Apprenticed as a 13-year-old to Seamus McGrath's yard at Sandyford on the southern outskirts of Dublin, the future champion jockey of Britain had already been riding racehorses for some five years. He spent only a year under McGrath's tutelage before his indentures were switched to Frenchy Nicholson at Prestbury near Cheltenham in 1967.

Frenchy Nicholson, so called because he had spent part of his early riding career at Chantilly, was a renowned schoolmaster of promising jockeys and, in addition to Pat Eddery and his own son David, a highly successful jump jockey and now trainer in his own right, he nurtured the careers of Paul Cook, Richard Fox, Tony Murray and Walter Swinburn. Eddery was not by any means an overnight success but the grounding he received from Frenchy Nicholson, a consummate horseman, provided the foundation for the skills which would ultimately enable him to become one of the world's great race riders.

Steve Cauthen had an equestrian background in Kentucky but unlike Eddery he was, in the best traditions of the theatre, an overnight sensation. Born in the small town of Walton on May Day, 1960, a fact still proudly recorded on the town's boundary signs, Cauthen's parents, Tex and Myra, had both dabbled in training on a modest scale. The embryo champion rider of both the United States and Britain could literally ride as soon as he could walk but the minimum age for a professional jockey in America is 16 so Steve was confined impatiently to riding work until that time came.

His first mount came just 11 days after his 16th birthday and his third ride in public was a winner. By the end of the following year—1977—Steve Cauthen was a household name in international racing circles having won prize-money totalling 6 million dollars. In 1978 he rode Affirmed to the Triple Crown, comprising the Kentucky Derby, the Preakness Stakes and the Belmont Stakes and, at just 18, was a self-made dollar millionaire. But, to make use of a truism of the Turf, racing is the greatest leveller and, after two early-season defeats in 1979, Cauthen lost the mount on Affirmed to Laffit Pincay and his decline was as rapid as his rise. A long sequence of losers cost him popularity with the fickle American racing public, his confidence ebbed

and the same people who had hailed him as a boy genius just a few months before dismissed the teenager as yesterday's man.

Robert Sangster, then Europe's leading owner and a Cauthen fan, stepped in to offer the American a contract to ride his horses trained by Barry Hills and Steve arrived in this country a month before his 19th birthday to begin his career all over again. The most casual glance at any racing record book covering the past decade shows at once how brilliantly he has succeeded. Champion jockey three times; winner of every English Classic race at least once, Steve Cauthen is admired and respected by professionals and fans alike in his adopted country.

Kim Tinkler (above left), wife of Malton trainer Nigel, and one of the most successful professional women riders.

Left: Immaculate turnout and perfect seats displayed by pupils of the British Racing School with tutors, in striped caps, fore and aft.

Learning the ropes (below). The British Racing School at Newmarket.

Apprentice Melody Town (right), a pretty girl and a promising jockey.

It may look like a Wild West Show (below right) but jockey John Carroll managed to win this race at Hamilton Park despite a slipping saddle. Appropriately enough, the horse is called Professional Touch.

In Cauthen and Pat Eddery, English racing is blessed with contemporaries of the highest international class. In fact, we can enjoy the benefits of an exceptional crop of jockeys: the veteran **Willie Carson**, now 47 but still riding with the zest and courage of a man much younger, together with that noted big-race specialist **Walter Swinburn**, to name but two.

Nor is English racing short of promising youngsters. **Frankie Dettori**, in his first season as senior jockey to the powerful Newmarket stable of fellow Italian Luca Cumani; the **Hills** twins, **Michael** and **Richard**, Pat Eddery's younger brother **Paul** and **Richard Quinn** all look to be riders with bright futures. Among the most promising apprentices, note has been taken of the stylish Yorkshire-based **Alan Munro** and **Dale Gibson**, and several others all striving to succeed in this ultra-competitive sport.

The emergence of a really talented female jockey is still awaited with anticipation. Women have made good headway as professional race riders in several other leading Turf nations, particularly the United States, but although quite a high percentage of youngsters undertaking tuition at the apprentice training schools are female, a top-quality girl jockey has still to make the breakthrough in Britain. Perhaps lack of opportunity rather than shortage of talent is the stumbling block.

141

The variety of Britain's racecourses is an essential element of the charm of the sport in this country. No major Turf nation can boast as many contrasting tracks as are to be found here. There is no stereotype, no physical or geographical pattern to racing in these crowded isles.

From Chester's tight, left-hand turns on a soup-plate level surface to the vast, undulating expanse of Epsom; from Sandown Park's stiff uphill finish to the downward plunge at Leicester, the contrasts are startling. Goodwood provides a magnificent Downland setting, Newmarket's Rowley Mile an austere heathland aspect. Urban tracks, country tracks, old-fashioned facilities and ultra-modern cantilever grandstands with every comfort for racegoers, British racing has them all. Seventeen courses are devoted exclusively to Flat racing in mainland Britain, a further 18 stage both Flat and National Hunt sport and there is a group of 25 at which only jump racing takes place.

Previous page: A good level break at Kempton Park in the autumn.

High summer at Newmarket. A big field about to leave the parade ring on the charming July Course.

To describe in any detail each and every British racecourse would occupy an entire volume but the following selection have earned their places by staging high-class sport over many years and becoming a part of Turf folklore. That is not to say many of the smaller tracks lack their attractions but the need to concentrate on this élite few should be self-explanatory.

Ascot is home of the annual Royal Meeting, one of the greatest concentrations of blue-blooded horseflesh in the world, and that midsummer highlight, the King George VI and Queen Elizabeth Diamond Stakes. Since 1987 the Berkshire course has also staged the Festival of British Racing meeting in late September, a single-day fixture offering the greatest amount of prize-money in the country for one programme.

Until 1939 Ascot staged only four days' racing each year but the use of the Royal course has greatly increased in the post-war period. A massive modernization programme took place there in 1961 when new grandstands were erected. Four years later Ascot opened its steeplechasing track to give all-year-round use of this splendid course which is now among the most popular in the country.

The Ascot track is right-handed and just over fourteen furlongs in circumference with a mile long straight track joining the round course three furlongs from the finishing post. It provides a severe test and horses of doubtful stamina rarely win there.

Ascot owes its very existence to Queen Anne who first sanctioned racing there. To this day the Monarch remains Ascot's owner and Royal pageantry forms a vital part of the scene there, particularly at the big June meeting. King George IV started the horse-drawn procession down the course before racing on each day of the Royal meeting, a custom which still delights the huge crowds who flock to Ascot Heath every summer.

The King George VI and Queen Elizabeth Diamond Stakes, started as recently as 1951 and run in July, is now Ascot's most valuable event. Such outstanding horses as the Triple Crown winner Nijinsky (1970), Mill Reef (1971), Shergar (1981), Dancing Brave (1986) and Nashwan (1989) owe part of their lasting fame to having won this great mid-summer prize. The French mare Dahlia (1973–74) remains the only horse to land the King George twice.

Arguably the most famous racecourse in the

Hamilton Park, on the southern outskirts of Glasgow, and the so-called Edinburgh track, actually located to the east of the Scottish capital at Musselburgh, are Britain's most northerly Flat courses. Ayr, Scotland's premier track, is the most westerly while that furthest east is Yarmouth on the Norfolk coast. Newmarket is not only the largest racecourse in Britain but covers the greatest area of any racing facility in the world. Chester's historic Roodee circuit is Britain's smallest.

Right: Unsaddling after the 1988 Royal Hunt Cup at Ascot.

Below: Persian Heights and Pat Eddery sweep to victory in 1988's St James's Palace Stakes before a huge Royal Ascot gallery.

The Royal procession at Ascot (left), a piece of English sporting heritage which delights visitors from all over the world.

The ring at Salisbury (above) with plenty of business for the ranks of bookmakers.

Left: A crowded paddock at Salisbury. Informal and relaxed, the Wiltshire track provides spectacular views from its perch on the Downs.

Above right: Longchamp's parade ring offers a perfect view for racegoers making a last-minute check on the well-being of their selections.

Lush and lovely Longchamp (right), the superb racecourse in the Bois de Boulogne, close to the heart of Paris.

Following pages: More than half a million spectators watch the Derby at Epsom every June. This scene was pictured on the 200th anniversary of the first running.

world, **Epsom** lies high on the Surrey Downs, just 15 miles (24km) from central London, is left-handed with uncompromising gradients and adverse cambers. Its great reputation relies on the fact that the Derby and Oaks are staged there and the long histories of those fabled races are interwoven into the very fabric of Epsom.

The original Epsom grandstand was constructed in 1829 and remained in use until 1927. Its replacement, now totally inadequate, is shortly to be demolished and a new structure, part of a wide-ranging modernization scheme, is expected to be undertaken within the next two years. Epsom has long needed improved facilities in order to provide a setting worthy of

147

Previous page: The Knavesmire during August's Ebor fixture. The magnificent and historic York course is renowned for the warmth of its welcome.

A sunny October day on Newmarket's Rowley Mile course (right).

A rural setting for racing at Folkestone (far right), near the Kent coast.

Below: King Charles II, an early enthusiast for racing at Newmarket, would be surprised by the modern-day stands.

Below right: An evening meeting at Sandown Park racecourse at Esher in Surrey, well supported all the year round by London racegoers.

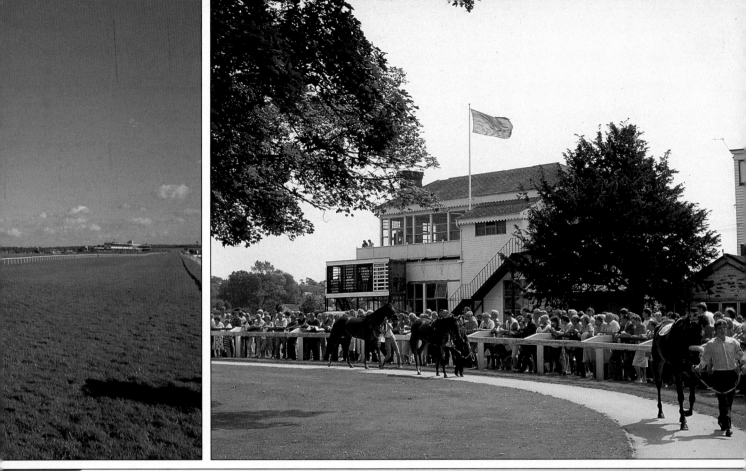

The parade ring at Doncaster (above), traditional home of the St Leger, is located in front of the grandstand.

Evening fixtures at Windsor's Thames-side track always attract big crowds (top right, centre).

Welney and Gary Carter pictured winning the Rokeby Farm Mill Reef Stakes at Newbury (above right, centre), one of the most popular courses in Southern England.

Yarmouth races (above, far right) provide a popular day out for summer visitors to the Norfolk resort.

Right: Parading before the Tote Diamond Jubilee Ebor Handicap at York.

Glorious Goodwood (far right), that unique setting overlooking the gentle slopes and woodland of West Sussex.

Previous page: A thrilling finish to Goodwood's 1989 King George Stakes, with the sprinters racing past the cantilever grandstand, a construction which enraged some traditionalists.

Dirt-track racing in England for the first time on October 30, 1989 (above). Lingfield Park stages the innovation on an all-weather surface designed to prevent cancellations during the winter months.

They're off! Gerry Cranham's ability to spot the unusual angle is perfectly illustrated by this starting-stalls study at Lingfield Park (right).

the Derby, that most celebrated of all horseraces.

It would be invidious to single out just one Derby and one Derby winner in this brief summary but perhaps the greatest of all Derby Days in terms of public acclaim came in 1896 when the Prince of Wales won the great race with his colt Persimmon. The extent of public rejoicing was extraordinary and the Royal owner mobbed by his adoring subjects. The scenes witnessed that afternoon nearly a century ago were never to be repeated, even when Diamond Jubilee (1900) and Minoru (1909) carried the Royal colours to further Derby triumphs.

Goodwood is the 'garden party' course situated on the Duke of Richmond and Gordon's

estate near Chichester in West Sussex, and enjoys the reputation of being the most attractive of British tracks. Right-handed and undulating, this singular course makes unusual demands on runners but provides a relaxed and sociable atmosphere for racegoers. In more leisurely times the Glorious Goodwood fixture in late July was said to signal the conclusion of the London 'season'.

Racing began at Goodwood in 1801 but the course offered only modest fare during its early days and it was not for a further quarter-century that Goodwood became fashionable with the landed gentry. These days Goodwood stages far more racing and despite its comparative inaccessibility is vastly popular with the public at large. The most valuable of its races now is the Group I Sussex Stakes, run over a mile at the Glorious Goodwood meeting. This is the richest rewarded of its type in Europe and regularly attracts the cream of eight-furlong specialists from France and Ireland in addition to those trained in this country.

From Petite Etoile in 1959 to Zilzal 30 years later, the Sussex course has provided a sequence of high-grade winners including any number of previous scorers in the 1,000 and 2,000 Guineas. Watching such brilliant animals perform in summer sunshine and in Goodwood's lush Downland setting is one of British racing's finest sights.

Newmarket has long been dubbed the Headquarters of British Flat racing. Looked upon as the home of the Jockey Club, although, these days, the administrative centre is in London's West End, Newmarket has two racecourses—the Rowley Mile and the Summer or July Course—and is also the country's largest training centre. The history of Newmarket as a racing and training town has been discussed in the opening chapter but a detailed description of the actual courses is called for since this corner of the Fens is the virtual birthplace of organized and disciplined horseracing in Britain.

The so-called Rowley Mile, used in the spring and autumn, actually runs straight for ten furlongs. The Guineas races, first of the season's Classics, take place over the final eight furlongs of this track. Its entire length is used for the major late-season event, the Dubai Champion Stakes. Races of 12 furlongs and longer start beyond an ancient earthwork feature known as the Devil's Dyke and join the straight course at the 10 furlong from home marker.

The Summer Course, used from June to August, has a straight mile while longer races start on the Cesarewitch course and turn right-handed into that straight by the eight-furlong start. The six-furlong July Cup, one of Europe's top sprint championship events, is the major race staged on the Summer Course.

Although the two courses adjoin they are very different in character. The Rowley Mile has a somewhat austere outlook, often with near-Siberian winds while the Summer Course, with its tree-lined paddock and agreeable atmosphere, is ideal for watching mid-season sport in a far more relaxed fashion.

However, no matter which of Newmarket's courses are in use, visitors can be assured of top-notch racing among the most expert crowd to be found anywhere. The little town of Newmarket eats, breathes and sleeps horses and very few of its inhabitants can remain aloof from this driving force.

Together with Doncaster, **York** is the centre of racing in Yorkshire. England's largest county has room for no fewer than nine courses but most racing regulars would rate York's venerable Knavesmire track the pick and many would nominate it as among the best in the whole country. The May and August fixtures—the

Hamilton Park (above), located on the southern outskirts of Glasgow, provides homely but competitive sport for Scottish enthusiasts.

Right: Up the hill with a furlong left to cover at Hamilton.

Previous page: A view of racing at York's August meeting taken from a vantage point high in the stand. The rows of candy-striped marquees in the background are used for corporate entertaining.

latter normally known as the Ebor Meeting in honour of the old-established handicap of that title—form the backbone of racing at York. The spring fixture features informative Derby and Oaks trials in the Dante Stakes and the Musidora Stakes while in August, in addition to the Ebor, there are such notable races as the Juddmonte International, the William Hill Sprint Championship, the Gimcrack Stakes and the Great Voltigeur Stakes.

That last named race celebrates the exploits of Lord Zetland's 1850 Derby and St Leger winner Voltigeur who ran a match race against The Flying Dutchman, the 1849 winner of those same two Classics, on the Knavesmire which contem-

Above: Turns are tight at Laytown and also-rans can get sand kicked in their faces.

Left: The paddock at Laytown Strand, north of Dublin, where racing takes place on the seashore – the state of the tide permitting.

A section of the expectant crowd thronging the Curragh on Budweiser Irish Derby day (far right).

porary reports claim was watched by a crowd of more than 100,000 people. Voltigeur lost by a length which makes one wonder just why the modern-day York event was not titled the Great Flying Dutchman Stakes?

York's long history as a racecourse and the high quality of the horses competing there contribute to the continued popularity of this fine track. Benefiting from outstanding management, the Knavesmire prides itself on a warm welcome for racegoers and few who visit the course fail to return on subsequent occasions. York is left-handed and flat, two miles in total length with a home straight five furlongs long. It rates as one of the fairest tests of the racehorse and there are rarely valid excuses for those beaten.

Other high-quality southern courses include Sandown Park and Newbury while Haydock Park, located halfway between Manchester and Liverpool, has made great improvements in recent years to join the elite of northern tracks.

Evening meetings during the summer months now play an important role in attracting racegoers and the Thames-side course at Windsor is specially well-supported. But outmoded legisla-tion prevents Licensed Betting Offices from remaining open to cater for off-course backers during the evenings so revenue is lost to the Betting Levy.

Racing on all-weather artificial surfaces has recently started at Lingfield Park in Surrey and the Nottinghamshire course at Southwell. It is, as yet, too early to make an accurate assessment of how successful and how popular this type of racing will prove to be in the long term but the experiment has full Jockey Club support and, although strongly opposed by some strident traditionalists, will at least assist in boosting returns both through the turnstiles and the Levy.

Racing, it must never be overlooked, exists not for the profit of a few wealthy owners but as a public entertainment. Britain has a unique resource in these widespread and differing venues which are unmatched in any other country. This multiplicity of environments and experiences must be cherished as a national treasure.

Racing in industrial South Yorkshire. Old-established Pontefract cannot claim to be England's most picturesque track, but provides consistently good sport.

RACECOURSES OF GREAT BRITAIN AND IRELAND

KEY

● Flat only

□ Flat and Jumps

HOW RACING WORKS

The relationships between the various bodies which administer racing have come about through historical accident, rather than any logically determined plan, and consequently the powers and responsibilities within the various aspects of the sport are often sketchily delineated.

The Jockey Club is synonymous with the administration of racing, and the Club has absolute power, incorporated by Royal Charter in 1970, to administer the rules and structure of racing. As we have seen in our opening chapter, the Club is the oldest horseracing authority in the world. Candidates, theoretically chosen for their knowledge of the sport, are proposed and seconded by members. Historically it has been a repository for some of the less energetic members of the aristocracy, but the past 25 years have brought a significant change in attitude.

As racing has expanded, and moved from a parochial pastime to an international business, the Jockey Club has responded—too slowly in the eyes of the progressives, but with a speed which would have been unthinkable 30 years ago.

The Jockey Club has more influence than any other racing organization, and considerable power. So how does it exercise that power? It is responsible for licensing all trainers and riders, both professional and amateur, and it determines jockeys' fees. It registers owners, ownership syndicates and companies, jockeys' valets, stable employees, equine swimming pools and stables. It also administers the Conditional Jockeys' Scheme for young riders.

It is responsible for the integrity of the sport and monitors the appointment of racecourse stewards, in addition to employing stewards' secretaries (the English equivalent to stipendiary stewards), handicappers, starters, judges and security staff, together with racecourse inspectors, doctors and vets.

The Club has four important committees for the administration of the sport. The Deputy Senior Steward chairs the Administration and Finance Committee and is responsible for the employment, salaries and welfare of the Club's licensed officials. Historically, they have been poorly paid as a consequence of almost being required to benefit from an army pension before appointment. In recent years salary levels have increased, although not necessarily to match the levels of responsibility discharged by officials such as handicappers and stewards' secretaries. These men, together with the Racecourse Security team, act as a police force, ensuring that the

Rules of Racing are adhered to, and that those who seek to benefit from breaking them are punished.

The Licensing Committee requires all trainers, jockeys and apprentices to sign an annual undertaking to abide by the Rules of Racing and breaches can result in withdrawal of licences. All new applicants are vetted by the Licensing Committee. A young trainer setting out on his or her chosen career will be subject to a searching interview by the Committee, and a Jockey Club inspector will visit their stables to ensure that

Previous page: A general view of the Tote's betting headquarters in Lancashire.

Jockey Club public relations manager David Pipe (right).

Below left: Clinical calm in the central computer room at Weatherbys.

Dr Michael Allen (below right), chief medical consultant to the Jockey Club.

Bottom right: The official day-to-day history of British racing is contained in the Racing Calendar. Some of these volumes are nearly 250 years old.

Below: Every horse in training must have a registered name and 'passport' for identification purposes, a massive undertaking for Weatherbys staff at the Wellingborough administration centre.

amenities reach the required standard. A minimum of 12 horses is needed before a training licence can be granted.

The Disciplinary Committee consists of highly experienced stewards, many of whom have ridden in amateur races. They deal with appeals against disqualifications at racecourses, or with more serious cases in the first instance. There is appeal from the Disciplinary Committee's findings to the Stewards of the Jockey Club, but beyond that appellants have recourse only to the courts. No Jockey Club disciplinary decision has been tested in court. Such is the burden of proof required at disciplinary hearings (at which defendants can be legally represented) that the likelihood of a decision being overturned outside the jurisdiction of the Jockey Club is minimal. However, the difficulty of proving to an acceptable degree of certainty that, say, a jockey is guilty of not trying to win on a horse, means that many who infringe the rules go unpunished although 'off the record' they might be warned as to their future conduct.

The Race Planning Committee has several responsibilities, including the management of the Pattern, that is, the progression of Group races for the best horses throughout a season (see the next chapter). This is a logically determined framework of races, but is based on the requirements of horses bred from a stock of stallions and mares a century ago. The subsequent influence of the more precocious American breed has altered both the type of horse raced in Britain and the methods of training. The traditional concept of a two-year-old being prepared for the top juvenile races and then being trained for all the season's Classics for which it was qualified, is becoming anachronistic.

The soaring value of stallions has ensured that for the past 20 years very few Thoroughbred colts contest all three Classics. A single defeat can detract substantially from a potential stallion's value, and the careers of most top-class racehorses are carefully nurtured.

The Pattern does change, but not much faster than the evolution of the world around it. Occasionally, inspired attempts to stage valuable new races are made, but they almost always conflict with the established Pattern and rarely progress beyond preliminary discussion. Race planning, in terms of the annual calendar of meetings, is a critical function. The Festival meetings normally place themselves, but there is considerable discussion and bargaining before the list of fixtures is finally decided.

In 1989 the Stewards of the Jockey Club decided that, in order to provide racing on winter days when traditional meetings had been cancelled, they would grant licences to two courses, Lingfield and Southwell, to build all-

weather tracks. The Club not only discussed the idea in embryo, but sanctioned tests and reports, took evidence from those who had experimented with the various artificial surfaces in use round the world and then planned the first series of all-weather meetings in the autumn and winter of 1989–90. The Jockey Club was responsible for all-weather racing from conception to inception.

In addition to wielding power in other important racing bodies, the Jockey Club is a major proprietor of racecourses. Through Racecourse Holdings Trust it owns or manages nine of the sixty tracks in the country: Aintree, Cheltenham, Haydock Park, Market Rasen, Newmarket Rowley Mile, Newmarket July, Nottingham, Warwick and Wincanton. Consequently, through this wholly-owned subsidiary, it wields considerable influence in the Racecourse Association.

The Jockey Club owns 4,000 acres of land at Newmarket, 2,500 of which are devoted to

Left: The blood-typing department at Newmarket's Animal Health Trust Laboratory.

Below left: Michael Hancock (right), the Jockey Club's senior Judge, testing a new colour photo-finish monitor.

Nick Lees (bottom left), Newmarket's Clerk of the Course.

Jockey Club starter Judy Grange (below).

174

Right: The Animal Health Trust laboratories at Newmarket provide modern aids to veterinary science. This picture shows an equine patient undergoing an X-ray of his near hind leg.

Charlie Toller (below), Clerk of the Course at Chester, stands proudly in front of the new grandstand, built to replace the previous building destroyed by fire.

John Smith (below right), appointed Clerk of the Course at York in 1988.

Morag Chalmers (bottom right), Europe's first woman Clerk of the Course when appointed to Hamilton Park.

racing, the remainder being farm land, woods and tenanted studs. Newmarket Estates Ltd manages this land for the benefit of racing at Newmarket. The day-to-day administration of the sport is delegated to Weatherbys, secretaries to the Jockey Club since 1770. Weatherbys has acted on a contractual basis since 1970, having handed over the copyright of racing information to the Jockey Club in 1952.

Weatherbys' traditional image of a quill-pen company has only recently been buried beneath substantial investments in new technology. Computers now handle the detailed *minutiae* of racing, from the entries and runners to the historical records of the Stud Book.

The Information Technology Department services the principal operational divisions of

Above: A combination of ultra-modern and traditional. Visual display units fronting a manually-operated results board at Tote betting HQ.

Above right: Presenter Richard Pitman prepares his script for an SIS studio telecast.

Right: Sporting and Racing Ltd's well appointed licenced betting office in Putney.

Weatherbys. Racing Administration is the largest department, and it broadly controls all British horseraces, some 6,000 a year, including the collection of entry fees and the distribution of prize money. It is the record keeper of all owners, trainers, jockeys and horses, and constantly updates the central database as changes of ownership, colours or stables are registered. It also sanctions the naming of racehorses.

In conjunction with Raceform, a private company, Weatherbys publishes form books which record the full result of each race. The pedigrees of all Thoroughbred racehorses are kept by Weatherbys on a computer and every four years they publish the *General Stud Book*. By creating and maintaining the most comprehensive historical database on British racing, Weatherbys not only services the racing industry, but issues several technical books for the Jockey Club, including those which detail each racing fixture.

The company also publishes the *Racing Calendar*, a weekly which records all official meetings of the Club, alterations to rules, inquiries held by race-meeting stewards, and details of all registrations and changes. Before 1988 it carried lists of entries for all races, but in that year the system was radically altered to accommodate entry at the five-day stage for most races, taken by telephone or facsimile machine, and the *Racing Calendar* now carries the entries and weights for

only the most important races of the season, for which the entries sometimes close months in advance.

While the Jockey Club controls the Rules of Racing and has widespread influence, it has little financial power. For the last full year, the Club's income was just over £8 million, most of which came from the Horserace Betting Levy Board, a government administered body which collects a percentage of betting revenue, and distributes it to the benefit of racing.

Racecourses have several sources of income, one of which is from daily grants made by the Levy Board, which was established in 1961. When betting shops and betting tax were introduced, it was decided that a proportion of betting turnover should be returned to the sport. Off-course punters are charged 10 per cent of a bet, which can be paid as one-tenth of the stake, or one-tenth of the winning returns. Of this, 8 per cent is taken by the government in betting tax, and a proportion of the remainder paid to

Michael Webster (above), Clerk of the Course at Epsom and Kempton Park, in his Derby day finery.

Kenneth Brown (left), the senior Jockey Club starter.

David McHarg (below left), Scottish racing supremo. 'Six feet five inches of Caledonian determination.'

Above right: A rudimentary vantage point for Irish Turf Club officials at the Curragh.

Don Cox (right), General Manager at Doncaster.

the Levy Board. The rate is discussed annually by the Levy Board and the bookmakers' representatives. On some occasions the negotiations have been placid, on others they have degenerated into a public argument which, ultimately, has been settled by the Home Secretary. The Levy discussions of 1988 brought one of the most vociferous disagreements, and when judgement was made by the Home Secretary in the following spring, it was generally agreed that the bookmakers had won on points.

In the early days of the Levy Board, the Jockey Club believed the revenue was its for the spending, but George Wigg, a Labour Cabinet Minister, was determined that the money raised from punters should be dispensed for a wider benefit.

The constitution of the Levy Board is finely balanced, with a chairman and two members appointed by the Home Secretary broadly to represent the interests of the punters, three members appointed by the Jockey Club, one of whom is the chairman of the Horserace Advisory Council, a non-legislative forum for the major interests of the sport. The chairman of the

Horserace Totalizator Board (Tote) and the chairman of the Bookmakers' Committee also have seats on the Levy Board.

In 1989 the Levy Board anticipated an income approaching £40 million, which it is required to spend on improving the breed, running the National Stud, the advancement of veterinary science, and the improvement of horseracing in general. About 40 per cent of the Levy Board's income is used to boost owners' prize-money levels. Individual grants are made to racecourses, with the emphasis on raising the minimum prizes. In return for this disbursement, the Jockey Club's annual fixture list is framed to maximize betting opportunities and thus boost Levy income, although this is not necessarily to the benefit of the racegoer.

Because betting shops are not allowed to remain open for evening racing, off-course turnover for such meetings is relatively low yet attendances are high, reflecting the requirements of the paying customer. The Jockey Club, the Levy Board and many other associated bodies have urged the government to introduce Sunday racing for the sport's benefit, but legislation to permit betting shops to remain open for evening racing would bring a much more immediate financial reward.

The Levy makes a significant contribution for what is officially described as the 'integrity of racing', ranging from dope testing to the costs of the Jockey Club security department. The Horseracing Forensic Laboratory is not only

Above: 'Room for one more!' The computer record bank at the Tote's central credit operation in Wigan.

Above left: Sophisticated equipment plays a part in beaming television pictures and commentary from racecourses to betting shops nationwide. This picture shows a Satellite Information Services engineer working in the lavishly appointed studio suite at their North London headquarters.

Left: Tote credit clients having their bets recorded. Michael Dillon (below left), public relations officer to the Ladbrokes bookmaking empire.

Right: Trainer and gambler Barney Curley in conversation with Victor Chandler, a leading rails bookmaker.
The Tote betting shop at Chester racecourse (above right).

Previous page: Salisbury, where racing has taken place since the Middle Ages.

responsible for carrying out the post-race urine tests to ensure that no horse has been administered a 'non-normal nutrient', but also carries out similar tests for other racing authorities and undertakes research programmes.

The Animal Health Trust is presently involved with several laboratories, including some abroad, to find effective vaccines against the various types of equine viruses. These not only affect a horse's racing performance, but equine herpes is detrimental to the health of pregnant mares, and frequently results in abortion. During 1989 the Levy Board supported

some 42 separate research projects, not only at the Animal Health Trust but at a dozen other locations, mostly British universities.

The Board makes interest-free loans to racecourses that wish to modernize facilities for racegoers, and some racecourses are prepared to forego the daily grant to hold a meeting, preferring the money to be saved in a capital account which can be used for redevelopment. The Board also funds point-to-point meetings, the craft of farriery, and apprentice training at the British Racing School, Newmarket. It makes grants available to training areas for improvements such as all-weather gallops. It wholly finances the Horseracing Advisory Council, a body used by the Jockey Club and Levy Board to provide an effective channel of communication between them and the many sectors of the industry.

Racecourse Technical Services is a wholly-owned subsidiary of the Levy Board. It provides a full range of technically-based services for the sport, including video camera patrols, starting stalls, and photo-finish equipment. Like the Horseracing Forensic Laboratory, RTS has begun to sell its services to outside clients.

The Levy Board manages the training grounds at Epsom and owns three racecourses, Epsom, Sandown and Kempton, under the umbrella of United Racecourses, a wholly-owned subsidiary of the Metropolitan and Country Racecourse Management and Holding Ltd.

In less than 30 years, the Levy Board has distributed its share of punters' betting turnover to give horseracing a much-needed facelift, in some cases paying directly or indirectly for services which previously had been funded by the Jockey Club or the racecourses. Many have observed that the relationship between the Jockey Club and the Board seems a little incestuous, but the influence of Lord Wigg in thwarting the Jockey Club's desire to control the levy from punters has been at least partially successful.

Prize-money comes from owners' entry fees and Levy Board contributions, but a proportion is received from racecourses. Their principal revenue has traditionally been receipts through the turnstiles, but nowadays they have various other sources of income. One of these is sponsorship, which now accounts for 23 per cent of the £23.5 million of prize money available in 1988, a proportion which has doubled in the past decade. Advertising hoardings and advertisements in racecards are also popular sources of income, while the more prestigious racecourses benefit from fees paid by the BBC and Channel 4 to televise the best meetings.

Recently, two more important sources of revenue have been created, from the coverage of racing by Satellite Information Services (SIS) and from premium-rate telephone services providing live commentaries. Until the mid-1980s, betting shop patrons listened to an audio commentary provided by Extel, the news and sports agency. Commentary fees were paid to racecourses, but were considered by many to be inadequate.

The Racecourse Association (RCA) represents the interests of the nation's 60 racetracks, and has a central secretariat run by a chairman and a chief executive. Three registered boards represent the North, Midlands and South but reaching binding agreement with so many individuals, often of widely differing requirements, is no simple task. The needs of Ascot and Sandown are sometimes far removed from those of Plumpton and Bangor.

Satellite Development Services was set up by bookmakers in the early 1980s to explore the possibility of transmitting live televised racing into betting shops. Every steward and punter knew that satellite was coming eventually but racing had no great sense of urgency to meet the challenge after two decades of innovation. The betting shops had been a part of the High Street for 20 years and during that time off-course bookmakers, rather than any other section of the racing community, made substantial profits. The four major chains—Ladbrokes, Hills, Corals and Mecca—backed SDS and when the racecourses eventually woke up to the potential, the

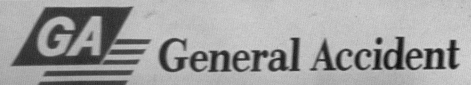

General Accident

Above: Nashwan (Willie Carson) winning the 1989 General Accident 2,000 Guineas from Exbourne (white cap), Danehill (centre) and Markofdistinction.

Right: Sir Harry Lewis beats Naheez at the Curragh. See if you can guess the title of the race!

Pat Firth (below right), Doncaster's Clerk of the Course.

Top left: The irrepressible Ras Prince Monolulu, the John McCririck of his day.

Rod Fabricius (left), Goodwood's Clerk of the Course, makes use of modern communications technology.

A fistful of notes for some lucky punter (below left).

bookmaker-backed company, now called Satellite Information Services, had such a lead over any potential rival that the result of the battle for the contract was a foregone conclusion.

Threatening to broadcast greyhound racing instead of horseracing, SIS soon saw off its rivals. It was much too late for racing to raise £50 million to boost Racecourse Technical Services to the position where RTS could beam live racing into the shops. With the whole of the racing estalishment firmly against the major bookmakers, seen popularly to be bleeding the sport as ruthlessly as legislation allowed, the RCA was under considerable pressure to find an alternative. It asked a consortium headed by Mercury Communications and GEC to bid, and the new competitor was verbally offered a contract under which racecourses would receive massive revenues and a major share of the com-

185

pany, but with no guarantee of large sums in the years immediately ahead.

To avert what seemed imminent defeat, SIS doubled its offer to a guaranteed minimum of £25 million over the first five years of operation and duly won the contract. By the end of 1989, all betting shops paying the requisite fees were receiving SIS, which transmits at least two meetings a day, and some were enjoying increases in turnover of 25 per cent.

British Telecom (and latterly Mercury Communications) has premium telephone lines which provide specialist services and since 1986 the public has been able to dial and listen to racecourse commentaries. Half-a-dozen competitors now provide this facility, some from the Extel racecourse team, that company's racing news agency having closed in the summer of 1988. This has proved another valuable source of revenue for the RCA, whose members are now enjoying greater prosperity than at any time during the past 30 years. As a result, gradually the antiquated grandstands are being replaced by modern structures, some more successful than others.

Racecourses charge course bookmakers for their pitches and receive a percentage of the turnover from betting shops on their premises. However, the most significant sums come from the Tote, the pool betting organization founded in 1929. Under the chairmanship of Lord Wyatt, the Tote has prospered in recent years, and a programme of computerization is almost complete. This allows cash and credit clients to bet at any meeting from any location at Tote odds, with their stakes registered in the pool up to the start of the race.

In its latest full financial year the Tote paid £4.3 million to racing, a figure that should be exceeded year on year for some time as the benefits of computerization boost turnover, and its importance as a powerful voice in racing will continue to increase. In 1988 the Home Secretary asked a merchant bank to prepare a feasibility study to investigate the privatization of the Tote. At the same time Sir Ian Trethowan, chairman of the Levy Board, expressed doubts that the Levy was a perfect and permanent system for funding the needs of racing and called for a government inquiry into the financing of the sport. Although the merchant bank had reported by the summer of 1988, the Home Secretary made

Above left: Corporate entertaining is big business on British racecourses as this impressive list of clients at the Chester May meeting clearly shows.

Left: Mrs George Walker, wife of the Brent Walker chairman, presenting a sponsor's trophy at Ascot, a scene repeated daily on racecourses throughout the country.

no announcement on either those findings or his decision on an inquiry, and in the autumn of 1989 the industry was still waiting.

In addition to the major forces of influence in racing, there are many associations which represent the individual sections of the industry including owners, trainers, jockeys and breeders. These are self-interested pressure groups, whose opinions are most often aired at meetings of the Horseracing Advisory Council, which has no executive power.

As so often happens when administrative structures are formed by accident rather than logic, the power in racing sometimes shifts according to personalities. With Lord Wyatt heading the Tote and Sir Ian Trethowan the Levy Board, their wide political contacts ensure that racing's voice is heard. There is an all-party Parliamentary Racing Committee consisting of MPs with an interest in the sport. When disputes occur they are lobbied from all sides, including the organizations representing bookmakers, of which the most powerful is BOLA, the Betting Office Licencees' Association.

The two issues the industry regards as most important in the medium term are Sunday racing and the opening of betting shops for evening racing. Campaigns to change the law to permit racing on Sunday are launched periodically, but have a formidable obstacle in the Lord's

Day Observance Society, and any change in government attitude is likely to follow more general legislation to relax the laws on Sunday trading. The closure of betting shops at 6.30pm is a legacy of the original Betting and Gaming Act of 1961, which legalized betting shops. But in an age when individuals can spend their evenings wagering on the speed of a greyhound or the spin of a roulette wheel, this particular aspect of betting shop legislation seems anachronistic.

Right: Jenny Sears tic-tacs for her bookmaker husband Derek at Goodwood.
Below: Commercial sponsorship provides a vital boost to prize-money levels. But sponsors expect high-level television exposure.

The Pattern of Racing is the overall design by which it is hoped to establish the best horses of each age and sex over the various distances. Although all major racing countries have their own patterns, they are to a considerable extent inter-dependent and the higher up the scale a race may be the more important this inter-dependence becomes. In spite of the fact that the Pattern is now arguably the dominant element in the present formal arrangement of racing, it has been in existence for less than 20 years.

For many seasons the only official group of races was that of the five Classics—the five most important races of the year confined to three-year-olds. These are the two Guineas races over a mile at Newmarket in the late spring, the Derby and the Oaks over a mile a half at Epsom in the summer and the St Leger over a mile and three-quarters at Doncaster in the autumn. Fillies may run in all five races, but colts may not contest the 1,000 Guineas or the Oaks.

When the 2,000 and 1,000 Guineas races joined the St Leger (first run in 1776), the Oaks (1779) and the Derby (1780 and over a mile for its first four runnings) in 1809 and 1814 respectively it soon became the greatest objective of an owner to have a colt or filly capable of winning the Triple Crown—a Guineas, the Derby or the Oaks and the St Leger—and that was just about all there was to the Pattern. Later the Derby winner was expected to contest the Ascot Gold Cup as a four-year-old. With far more courses in existence then than there are now and no body even remotely resembling the Jockey Club's Race Planning Committee of today the whole thing was very haphazard.

Clearly some semblance of order had to be brought into play and in 1965 the Jockey Club set up a committee, chaired by the late Duke of Norfolk, to investigate the pattern of racing with the intention of providing a balanced programme of high-class, non-handicap races for horses of all ages and over all distances throughout the season. Two years after the Norfolk Committee had completed its deliberations Lord Porchester (now Lord Carnarvon) chaired another panel, known as the Race Planning Committee, and in 1970 the authorities in France and Ireland joined those in Great Britain in devising a system to select the races which would be included in the four categories of Groups I, II and III and Listed races (which are, in effect, those of Group IV). At one time some of the most important handicaps were taken into the Listed category but that practice has now

been abandoned. The original report by the Duke of Norfolk's panel made the somewhat pompous observation that 'handicaps place a premium on mediocrity', and while such a comment should not pass unchallenged in relevant circumstances, the definition of a horse's superiority is arguably best reached via weight-for-age races.

In general terms those races in Group I can be regarded as of championship level importance; those in Group II are just below top level and those in Group III are stepping stones to higher things. The Pattern and the races in it are reviewed each year by the European Committee and there are frequent, even if not dramatic, changes to the status of many of the events. In 1986, for example, there were 20 races in Group I, 29 in Group II and 54 in Group III; for 1989 the respective figures were 23, 29 and 53. There were also 86 Listed races in 1989.

The Royal Ascot meeting in June provides good examples of how a race's status can vary over the years. The Gold Cup there has been the only one of the fixture's 24 races to hold Group I status since the Pattern was introduced in 1971. It was joined in 1987 by the St James's Palace and Coronation Stakes, but the King's Stand Stakes, elevated to the highest level two years after the

Pattern started, dropped back to Group II in 1987. This latter change was a piece of muddled thinking, namely that championship honours should not be judged in June. If the King's Stand Stakes may not hold Group I ranking in June, how may the Gold Cup? Other examples of Pattern changes from the four days of the Royal meeting are the promotion of the Queen Anne Stakes to Group II in 1983 and the relegation to Group III in the same year of the Coventry and Queen Mary Stakes for two-year-olds. The latter move met with widespread approval as the changing style of a racehorse's life and home training methods have meant that the two-year-old races at Ascot now have considerably less significance than in past years.

In the championship Group I races the horses meet strictly on weight-for-age and sex terms with no allowances or penalties. Further down the scale such conditions come into effect and a horse who has won a Group I race will almost invariably have to carry a penalty when he contests an event at a lower level, with the same applying to Group II winners in Group III races. This is where a weakness in the Pattern, or to be more precise, in the official status of some of the races in it, can be illustrated.

Although it retains Group I status, the Middle Park Stakes at Newmarket in October has lost much of its prestige in recent years and has been won by only one subsequent English Classic winner in that time. Even that colt, the 1979 2,000 Guineas victor Known Fact, took that prize only as the result of a disqualification. But because the Middle Park is still rated in the highest echelon victory in it attracts a Group I penalty when such conditions apply and very often its winner cannot either compete successfully at the highest level in subsequent seasons or carry the penalty against rivals who have not won in that sphere. It would be no major surprise to find the Middle Park dropped in grade in the near future and there is no doubt that the constant review and flexibility of the Pattern is one of many factors in its favour.

It is essential to give a proper series of

Previous page: Secreto and Christie Roche (nearer camera) beating El Gran Señor (Pat Eddery) for the 1984 Ever Ready Derby. Secreto was trained by David O'Brien, son of El Gran Señor's trainer, Vincent O'Brien.

Left: A close call in the 1989 William Hill Lincoln Handicap at Doncaster with Tyrone Williams scoring on the 20–1 chance Fact Finder, for Reg Akehurst's Epsom Stable.

Geoffrey Gibbs (top left), the senior Jockey Club handicapper, pictured on duty at Kempton Park.
The late Phil Bull (bottom left), founder of Timeform, in typically pugnacious pose.

opportunities to horses over all ranges of distance, and though the sprinters lost the King's Stand in 1987 they gained the Ladbrokes (formerly the Vernons) Sprint Cup at Haydock the following year. The introduction of the Festival of British Racing at Ascot in September 1987, resulted in the elevation to Group I of that day's Queen Elizabeth II Stakes.

Though some horses are undoubtedly flattered by winning Group I races and their connections later have to decide whether the prize-money and alleged status have been worth the diminution of their subsequent opportunities, it is unarguable that in general the penalty and allowance system through the Pattern works very satisfactorily. Take as an illustration the case of Warning, who was rated the top miler in Europe in 1988 after his success in the Queen Elizabeth II Stakes. His campaign the following season began in the Group II Juddmonte Lockinge Stakes at Newbury in May and Queen Anne Stakes at Ascot the following month. In

Above left: The French filly Ravinella (Gary Moore) swoops to land the 1987 General Accident 1,000 Guineas.

Left: Persian Heights (Pat Eddery) is first home in the 1988 York International, but was disqualified at a subsequent stewards' enquiry.

Below: The great French jockey Yves Saint-Martin pictured landing the 1976 1,000 Guineas on Flying Water. Saint-Martin won every English Classic and was champion jockey of his own country 15 times during a distinguished career.

Racing on the Rowley Mile course at Newmarket in 1988 (above). Green's Canaletto is shown beating Shalfleet for the Snailwell Maiden Stakes.

Luca Cumani's top-flight handicapper Fish n' Chips (right), pictured with Lester Piggott in the saddle.

Below right: Swiss Maid and Greville Starkey return from taking the 1978 Champion Stakes. Gillian Kelleway, wife of winning trainer Paul, is in the foreground.

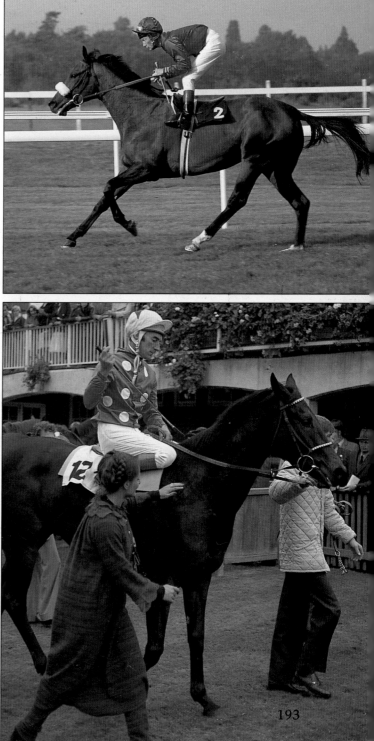

both he had to carry his Group I penalty, so that he had to give weight to all his opponents.

It is every owner's dream to own a horse who is the best of his vintage and capable of winning at Group I level. But as most horses never win a race of any sort and there are only just over 20 Group I races a year, such aspirations have to be tempered with realism and the pyramid-like structure of the Pattern is designed to give the less talented horses the chance of winning races at their own standard. The 23 Group I events are the apex of the pyramid; it then expands at the next level to take in the 29 from Group II, and below them are the 53 from Group III. After that come the 86 Listed events and as the pyramid steadily gets wider, on the next level are the major handicaps; below them are lesser weight-for-age races and the spectrum gradually broadens until at rock-bottom level are the really bad selling handicaps and maiden races. These seem designed to attract the worst horses in training and because there are so many horses which qualify for such a description these races almost always have plenty of runners.

By the time an owner or trainer has decided that the lowest level of competition is the only option open to them and their almost talentless horse, they will no doubt have tried higher targets along the way. Although, of course, by adopting Admiral Rous's somewhat cynical maxim of keeping themselves in the best company and their horses in the worst, some horsemen specialize in aiming their horse delib-

Above: Willie Carson drives Safawan (rails) home to win Goodwood's Schweppes Golden Mile from Serious Trouble (11), Mirror Black and Malevich.

Left: Very Adjacent (Dale Gibson) and Plain Fact (George Duffield) fighting out the finish of the 1989 Stewards' Cup. Very Adjacent, wearing a visor and an outsized sheepskin noseband, won by a short head.

A desperate finish to the 1989 Royal Hunt Cup (below left) sees True Panache (No. 9) and champion jockey Pat Eddery snatch the prize.

erately low and landing a major betting coup in the process. It is by no means unheard of for horses to improve greatly after running in sellers: the 1938 Oaks and 1,000 Guineas winner Rockfel actually finished eighth of 11 in a selling plate in her first race. Which brings us to the problem of handicapping.

There is, of course, no obligation for anyone to reveal to the Jockey Club's handicappers or, indeed to anyone else, how good their horse may be. 'Stopping'—preventing a horse from running on his true merit or from finishing as close up as he can—is against the Rules of Racing, but winning by narrow margins with the intention of making a horse look less good than he is has always been a totally acceptable ploy, even though the handicappers themselves may not always appreciate such a tactic.

It has become the fashion in recent years for expensive and blue-blooded horses from some of the major stables at Newmarket and Lambourn to win their early races at humble courses like Carlisle, Catterick and Leicester. These horses often start at long odds on and do not win by large margins from opponents who ought, on at least a theoretical basis, to be vastly inferior. The handicapper's dilemma is having to assess the winner on this very tenuous evidence and the problem has become all the greater since the rules were amended to allow a horse to be

given a handicap rating after just one race, as long as it has been a win. (Otherwise it is still compulsory for a horse to run three times before it can be handicapped.)

So Jockey Club officials are faced with having to give an official rating to a potentially very smart colt who has run (and won) only once in distinctly run-of-the-mill company but who has also been entered for one of the major handicaps later in the season. They are inevitably fighting in the dark and the best that can really be said for their efforts is that they are judicious guesswork. In such circumstances it is a great credit to the handicappers that their ratings prove as accurate as they do over the course of a season.

In recent years perhaps no one has played this particular game with more finesse and success than Luca Cumani. Although from the outset of his training career in Newmarket in 1976 Cumani has trained horses of Classic standard— he sent out Konafa to be second to Flying Water in the 1,000 Guineas in that first season and had three more Classic places the following year— his ability to spot a horse capable of winning a major handicap and keep that horse's ability under wraps was not long in being established.

In 1985, for example, the three-year-old colt Fish 'n' Chips made his third appearance of the season in the £1,108 Ennerdale Water Stakes for maidens at Carlisle on 5 June. Fish 'n' Chips had

Above: Steve Cauthen (left, in tartan) pushes the filly Cormorant Wood through to win the 1983 Dubai Champion Stakes.

Left: Cutting Blade (Cash Asmussen) returning to unsaddle after winning the 1986 Coventry Stakes. Successful trainer Lester Piggott (right) smiles his appreciation.

Lord Porchester (below left), clearly delighted that his colt Little Wolf has just won the 1983 Ascot Gold Cup.

been unplaced in two previous runs that season and at Carlisle won this insignificant race at 11–8 on by no more than two lengths and, according to the official form book, not especially easily. A fortnight later he won a considerably better event at Redcar before returning to Carlisle where this time he started at 5–1 on, his display earning the word 'easily' from the race-reader. It was on that sort of evidence that the colt had to be assessed for an all-aged handicap at Yarmouth. Here, in spite of 9st 9lb and a 5lb penalty, he was not extended to win and at the end of July he won the valuable Extel Handicap at Goodwood 'comfortably' after going off as 9–4 favourite in a field of 13. In under two months Fish 'n' Chips had moved up from winning a very modest race not all that impressively to taking one of the year's most competitive handicaps with his share of ease. The handicapper can be forgiven for having always seemed one step behind him, and the colt was even then not finished for later in the year he won a handicap at Ascot under 9st 7lb.

However, since the advent of the five-day entry system in 1989, it has become less easy to keep horses ahead of the handicappers. With the exception of some early closing major events like the Chester Cup, the Royal Hunt Cup, the Cambridgeshire and the Cesarewitch, race entries are made only five days before the event is due to take place and the handicappers, with the aid of computers based at each racecourse, are able constantly to revise their assessments of a horse's merits. In any case, it is almost inevitable that the handicapper will catch up one day with a horse who has been eluding him. Sometimes it is that which stops a horse's progress, but on other occasions the horse himself simply stops improving and many an owner or trainer will be heard to remark that it is much easier to go up the handicap than it is to come down it again. Handicappers are like elephants—they have long memories.

Outwitting the handicapper is just one part of a trainer's skill. Advancing a horse so that he can gain the much sought-after 'black type' for being placed in a Group race is another important target. Here again the Pattern comes into play. Once a horse has won his good handicaps his chances of doing so in the immediate future are almost bound to be limited for the reasons explained above, so the next step has to be to advance him in grade and to run in Listed and then proper Pattern company.

The significance of black type is that the races involved have been printed in that colour in sales catalogues. It has to look better to a potential buyer of a foal or a yearling or a broodmare if the achievements of its relations involve plenty of black printing, and it cannot be denied that sometimes the status of the race can be considerably greater than the merit of the performance required to earn black type from it.

It is a simple statement of fact—there is no disrespect intended—to say that racing in Italy and Germany is of a lower general standard than that in England, France and Ireland, though Irish racing seems at a somewhat low ebb just at the moment. Italy and Germany are, however, involved in the European Pattern and therefore have their Group races in the same way as the more powerful racing nations have theirs. All Group races carry black type when relevant and there is now an established rationale for British-trained horses in this country to try for Group III and Listed races on the Continent in the belief that those at home might be beyond them.

One of the best pieces of equine detective work in recent years was put up by Peter Walwyn for his filly Just Kala. One of the complications of taking horses to race overseas is that European countries are still inclined to adopt a protectionist policy and restrict a considerable number of their Group races to horses bred in their country; on the whole the lesser the status of the race the more likely this is to apply. Walwyn was seeking to advance the status of Just Kala after she had been a clear-cut winner of a maiden race at Epsom during Derby week. He took the view that moving her up into Listed company in England would be too much of a good thing, but after what must have been the result of hours poring over the European Pattern book, he came up with a suitable race at a track called La Teste-Arcachon, near Bordeaux in south-west France, hardly a popular stamping-ground for Lambourn-trained runners. Just Kala justified all her trainer's efforts by winning

Above right: the formidable combination of champion jockey Pat Eddery and Guy Harwood-trained Warning on their way to victory in the 1988 Sussex Stakes at Goodwood.

Right: Tyrnavos (Tony Murray) scores a shock success in the 1980 Irish Sweeps Derby at the Curragh.

Rounding Tattenham Corner (above) in the Ladas Maiden Stakes at Epsom's August fixture in 1989. Note how difficult it is to balance juveniles on this sharp left-hand bend.
Above right: The Gordon Stakes at Godwood in 1989, with Walter Swinburn forcing Warrshan to a narrow victory.
The magnificent Chester Cup (left), one of British racing's oldest trophies.

the first prize of £10,582, earning Listed status into the bargain. Later in the year, the filly finished fourth in the five-runner Group II Nassau Stakes at Goodwood, which shows how the insurance of the Bordeaux trip benefited from exploring the Pattern in depth.

If a horse has won at Group III the obvious move is to try him at the next level of competition in Group II. All the time those involved are finding out how good he may be and although almost every horse has to find his level sooner or later it is invariably an intriguing exercise watching their progress. Not all manoeuvres can be as successful as those involving Fish 'n' Chips or Just Kala, but a progressive horse can make amazing improvement in the course of a season.

It is claimed by the race's detractors that the Champion Stakes is not the reliable yardstick its Group I position suggests that it should be—and that at the end of October it comes too late in the year. Admittedly, it has produced its share of surprising results over the years, but it has also

been won in recent times by horses who began the season without such lofty aspirations. The fillies Swiss Maid and Cormorant Wood are examples of how a horse (particularly a filly) can improve at such a rate as to take almost everyone by surprise, and thus there is considerable incentive to keep trying to advance a horse up the merit ladder.

Inevitably there are plenty of examples of horses who have to travel in the other direction to enjoy any success. Many an animal starts the year at the highest level, with apparent justification for so doing, only to find the standard of competition too hot. He has to be dropped in class, sometimes more than once, before he can find a race to win, but the structure of the Pattern gives him every chance to do so at varying levels and at the same time enables those more dispassionately involved to assess his merits. The Pattern may not be perfect—in a sport as variable as racing it is unlikely that anything ever can be—but considering its complications it is conspicuously successful.

The International Classifications are the conclusions reached by the senior official handicappers of the five major racing nations in Europe—England, France, Ireland, Italy and Germany—as to which are the best horses to have raced in all or any of those countries during a particular year. Their opinions are by no means universally accepted and the horses involved quite frequently do not live up to them,

but the ratings are taken as the best available yardstick at the time. However sophisticated the means of identifying and evaluating the relevant information may be, there must be an element of opinion in any such exercise and no one's opinion is infallible.

The practice of annual official assessment of horses' merits is not new, though its expansion to include horses trained in other countries is a recent innovation. The idea had its origins in the British Free Handicap, which was first published in 1928 and dealt with the two-year-olds of that campaign. Horses were assessed down to a certain level of ability, usually with a range of about 21lb, and they were entitled to run in the Free Handicap at Newmarket's Craven meeting the following spring. There were corresponding lists in Ireland (the Madrid Free Handicap), in France (Handicap Optionel) and in the United States (Experimental Handicap), but it is only since 1977 that the three European racing powers have combined to publish their joint conclusions.

The Free Handicap was, of course, 'free' only in name. Although there was no initial entry fee—horses which were not considered good enough simply did not qualify—an acceptance fee had to be paid to take part and it has on several occasions been a good pointer to the season's subsequent winners of the Classics. In 1936 Pay Up went on to win the 2,000 Guineas; the following year Mid-day Sun went on to

Derby glory and more recently Honeylight, Petite Etoile, Mrs McArdy and Privy Councillor have followed that example. Other subsequent major race winners to have won the Free Handicap have been Wilwyn, Counsel, Faultless Speech, Port Merion and Moorestyle, but it has not fallen to a Classic winner since Mrs McArdy in 1977 and though it was opened up to horses trained outside Great Britain in 1980 as yet there has been no such challenger.

Corresponding with the Free Handicap, the Jockey Club's senior official used also to reveal his opinions about the older horses of the year and there was a race for them at the Guineas meeting at Newmarket. This has long been discontinued, however, and the ratings for horses aged three and more at the end of a season are now officially described as being for information only.

When the authorities in Great Britain, France and Ireland decided to launch the idea of International Classifications in 1977, it was agreed that the top-rated mark should be 100, with the margins between the highest-rated and those below giving clear indication of how far superior that horse was. Although that part of the system was discarded in 1985, the annual ratings are an authoritative, even if not always infallible, guide to the respective merits of one generation against another.

Under the practice of rating the best at 100, only one horse attained such distinction in official eyes: the brilliant 1981 Derby winner Shergar, whose sad fate less than two years later denied an outstanding racehorse the chance to establish just as high a reputaiton at stud. The one crop which did represent him included useful winners in Maysoon, Tashtiya and Dolka and who can say what might have happened afterwards? Incidentally, it is interesting to observe that Weatherbys, the keepers and compilers of the General Stud Book, appear not to believe that Shergar is dead. 'Left stud in 1983' is their version of things.

The nearest to Shergar under this system were the dual Prix de l'Arc de Triomphe winner Alleged and El Gran Señor, who won the 2,000 Guineas and the Irish Derby as well as being narrowly and controversially beaten at Epsom. They were rated at 98 (that is, 2lb behind Shergar), while Troy achieved 96 and Ile de Bourbon (at three and four), The Minstrel, Blushing Groom, Slip Anchor and Teenoso (at four) were assessed a pound lower. Perhaps inevitably no two-year-old achieved such a mark during the period under review and none was able to equal the 91 given to Tromos in 1978, the first year of juvenile ratings.

Since the ceiling of 100 was removed the handicappers have had considerably more

scope for manoeuvre and they have had no doubt that the outstanding racehorse they have seen in that time was Dancing Brave over a mile and a half. His successes in the Prix de l'Arc de Triomphe and the King George VI and Queen Elizabeth Diamond Stakes earned him a rating of 141. His success in the Eclipse Stakes earned a mark of 134 which, by coincidence, is the same figure as that earned by Shahrastani for his defeat of Dancing Brave in the Derby. To conclude, though, that because Dancing Brave at his best was assessed 7lb superior to Shahrastani at his then the former should have won the Derby is not a justifiable step. At their best there is no doubt, in the handicappers' joint view, which was the better colt, but this does not argue that the Dancing Brave who was beaten at Epsom was as good a horse as the Dancing Brave who won at Longchamp.

The highest mark achieved since Dancing Brave was by Reference Point in 1987 when he won the Derby and the King George. On that form he was considered to be 1lb superior to his Eclipse conqueror Mtoto, who rates 134 for that Sandown success, alongside Shahrastani and the nine and a half furlong-plus of Dancing Brave the year before. Compared with these, the best that the 1988 older horses can come up with is the mark of 133 given to Warning and earned no doubt by far and away the best performance of his career—his success in the Queen Elizabeth II Stakes at Ascot in September. As far as the panel was concerned, this was enough to rate him 2lb above the Arc first and second, Tony Bin and Mtoto. Next best was the disqualified York International 'winner' Persian Heights on 129, and it does not say too much for the cream of 1988 that it should be necessary to drop down below 130 in order to fill the first four places in the pecking order.

With the two-year-olds there is less variation in the top marks, no doubt at least in part because there is comparatively little evidence to use. Gone, probably for ever, are the days when the cream of juvenile talent was out by Ascot in June and certainly by Goodwood at the end of July. It is quite a thought that Reference Point is the only Derby winner of the past 12 years to have won a Group I race as a two-year-old. Reference Point's 1986 mark of 127 is the highest of any two-year-old over the past three seasons. That is 2lb higher than the figure awarded to High Estate for his 1988 form and to Warning and Ravinella, who could not be separated at the end of 1987. Though the handicappers' opinions are often the subject of stringent—and sometimes, it has to be said, pointlessly and boringly esoteric—criticism, the fact that Reference Point won the Derby and Ravinella the 1,000 Guineas, that on all subsequent form Warning would have won the 2,000 Guineas and that High Estate could not take part due to injury, suggests that the annual official conclusions are not as wide of the mark as some might have you believe.

The task facing the five-man panel—the experts from Germany and Italy joined in 1985—has become increasingly daunting over the years due to the constant increase in the number of horses in training and the number of races held. The fact that horses, particularly from England, now travel to race on the Continent has in many ways eased the burden of cross-relating the form of races in different countries, enabling horses trained in Italy and Germany to be listed in the two-year-old handicap for 1988. The talented German-trained five-year-old Acatenango was rated third behind Celestial Storm and Tony Bin in the four and upwards list for 1987.

All handicappers keep running lists of the horses they are required to assess. Thus they go into metaphorical battle with all the information available to them and to rate each horse is simply a question of reaching agreement among themselves. Sometimes it is rather cynically concluded among those not immediately involved that the highest mark for the two-year-olds operates on a 'Buggins' turn' system, with Britain, France and Ireland having the section leader on rotation, but this view does not stand up to serious inspection. No Irish-trained horse has been top here since El Gran Señor (128) in 1983.

There have been moves afoot for a while to include horses trained in the United States in the classifications and it seems likely that it will happen one day. The Anglo/Irish/French presence in major US races like those of the Breeders' Cup is now an established part of the season and already there may be enough points of contact for the best American horses to be included, making the ratings conspicuously more international. Incorporating those trained in New Zealand and Australia may be a rather more remote idea.

One of the occupational hazards of being a handicapper is that of being constantly accosted by trainers and owners saying that their horse has been given too much weight; if a man says that his horse is well handicapped there are those who fear for his sanity or wonder from what angle he is approaching what problem. As far as the classifications are concerned, the opposite case applies: the higher a horse is officially regarded the better pleased connections almost invariably are. They are already looking well into the future, with sale or stud value in mind. The opportunity to state in advertisements or in syndication brochures that their horse was officially rated better than others is one which no promoter would miss and such publicity for a horse is often accompanied by a Jockey Club or Timeform rating accentuating his best qualities. (It is, incidentally, a major tribute to Timeform and all involved with it since the late Phil Bull launched the idea more than 40 years ago that its ratings are accepted all over the world as being totally dispassionate and the result of disinterested analysis. Few commercial firms qualify for such comment.)

One area in which the inclusion of any such ratings might *not* be received with total enthusiasm is that of the sales catalogue. At the moment, as was indicated in the chapter on the Pattern of Racing, the only definition of a horse's level of talent is the use of black type for Group races. All you know from that is that the horse won or was placed in a race in one of the international groups. The vast number of such races in the United States tend only to bamboozle or confuse. Hence black type on its own can be said to be the truth as opposed to the whole truth.

To state in a catalogue that a horse won a Group III race tells a reader nothing more than

that. It is perfectly possible that to do so the horse in question had to beat just one totally outclassed opponent and that the exercise was little more than a walkover. Equally, if a horse is shown as having finished third in black-type company, it may have come third of three and been beaten out of sight by the other two. Facts are facts but they are worthy of elaboration in the interests of everyone except the vendor and, indirectly, the auctioneers who will receive more commission the higher the price of the sale. Although many horsemen carry an immense amount of detail in their heads and have immediate access to necessary sources, they cannot be expected to know every fact about every horse.

This is where the international ratings can be seen as the ideal means for indicating just how good any horse may be, and lower down the domestic scale the same principle can equally easily be applied. Alongside the list of the horse's best performances can be shown the mark he was given at the end of one, or some, or all his seasons' racing. Thus, instead of the mere

fact that the horse finished second in a Group II race at Longchamp, or won a Group I event at the Curragh, the catalogue will also display how highly he was regarded by the official assessors either at his best or at the end of a season. As has been made clear, the opinions which the panel produces are utterly objective and those without the intimate knowledge of the horse in question can thus easily obtain a realistic idea of his ability.

Such an idea would not please those who hope to dress up their offering with black type and no elaboration but if the information about a horse's realistic merit can be gained by lengthy study of the form book, there is no reason why it should not be much more readily available in the catalogue. The idea works perfectly well in both directions: it is just as possible for a man not to know how highly a horse has been officially rated as it is for him to be over-persuaded by the appearance of lines of black type which may not bear close examination.

The idea has been mooted in the upper echelons of the bloodstock market, but it has reached no further than that at present. Of course, it would involve more work for the catalogue compilers and technical details such as a cut-off date for ratings—any alterations can always be made clear at the time of sale as is the case today with other tangential matters—but there is no justifiable reason why it should not be adopted in the near future.

A Kempton Park traffic jam (below left) – little room for manoeuvre as the field for the Novair International Claiming Stakes turns into the straight.
Below: Super One, the blinkered horse second from right, comes late to land York's Yeardley Continental Rous Selling Stakes at the 1989 Ebor meeting. Super One was sold for 21,000 guineas at the subsequent auction.

GREAT HORSES, GREAT RACES

England's five Classic races for three-year-olds form the backbone of a domestic Flat season which stretches from mid-March to early November. The first two, the 1,000 Guineas and the 2,000 Guineas, the former for fillies only but the latter open to either sex, are each run over a mile on Newmarket's Rowley Mile course in the spring.

The 2,000 Guineas was inaugurated in 1809 with the fillies' event coming into being five years later. The Epsom Oaks, raced over one and a half miles for fillies only, was first run in 1779 while the Derby, over the same course and distance but open to both colts and fillies, started a year later. However, the season's final Classic, Doncaster's St Leger (one and three-quarter miles for both sexes) was founded in 1776. It is run in mid-September, just over three months after the Derby and the Oaks which take place on the first Wednesday and Saturday of June, respectively.

In support of these highly-valued and prestigious annual highlights of the Turf calendar come other major races which form part of the European Pattern system. Apart from the five Classics, English racecourses stage a further 18

Group I Pattern contests chief among which, in terms of prize-money values, are Ascot's King George VI and Queen Elizabeth Diamond Stakes, the Champion Stakes at Newmarket, Goodwood's Sussex Stakes, the Queen Elizabeth II Stakes (Ascot), the Juddmonte International (York), the Eclipse Stakes (Sandown Park) and the Coronation Cup (Epsom). Additionally, in 1989, British courses staged 29 Group II races and no fewer than 53 designated Group III.

There are now more (and more valuable) big-race occasions that stimulate increased betting

Previous page: Nashwan shows his seven-league stride in winning the 1989 Ever Ready Derby. Willie Carson looks to be hanging on for dear life.

Right: Nijinsky and Lester Piggott being led in after completing the 1970 Triple Crown. The great Irish-trained colt was the first horse to win the 2,000 Guineas, Derby and St Leger for 35 years.

Below: Another Derby for the peerless Lester Piggott, this time on The Minstrel (left) in 1977.

Above: Greville Starkey gets a great run out of Shirley Heights (rails) to score his only Derby success. Starkey retired at the conclusion of the 1989 season.

Above right: The great Mill Reef (Geoff Lewis) spreadeagles his field for a 1971 Derby triumph.

Right: Dancing Brave and Pat Eddery win the 1986 Prix de l'Arc de Triomphe, ahead of perhaps the best field ever assembled for the great Longchamp race.

Far right: The 1981 Derby is a one-horse cakewalk for the Aga Khan's Shergar.

The great French-trained stayer Sagaro (below, right) achieved a hat-trick of Ascot Gold Cup wins in the mid-1970s with Lester Piggott in the saddle each time. This picture shows Sagaro scoring, hard-held, in 1976.

A battle royal for the 1975 King George VI and Queen Elizabeth Diamond Stakes (below, far right) with the Derby winner Grundy (Pat Eddery) just having the measure of Joe Mercer's mount Bustino, hero of the previous season's St Leger.

turnover and racecourse attendances. An estimated 500,000 people attend Epsom Downs on Derby Day. Compare this with attendances at other famous sporting events: the Epsom crowd is almost six times the figure for an FA Cup Final at Wembley Stadium; tenfold the attendance at a Lord's Test match between England and Australia or the figure achieved on finals day at the Wimbledon Lawn Tennis Championship.

The Derby's mystique and tradition affect people who normally hold no more than a passing interest in the so-called Sport of Kings. Derby Day is singular and although the Epsom race is impersonated throughout the world it manages to remain essentially inimitable.

Epsom provides a stern test for contestants bidding for Derby or Oaks immortality. The Classic course, perched high on the north face of the Surrey Downs is, in the words of the great American jockey Bill Shoemaker, 'unlike any other track horses are asked to race over'. Hilly, twisting and cambered, it follows the natural

contours of the Downs, essentially unaltered since the races were devised more than two centuries ago. To reach the 12-furlong start the runners must cross a main road on which the traffic has to be stopped, a procedure that leaves foreign visitors to the Derby scratching their heads.

To win a Derby or an Oaks a horse needs to possess an unusual combination of speed, stamina and adroitness together with courage. The standard of even great races like these is, of course, variable but very few horses outside the highest class can expect to gain a victory in either of Epsom's top events. Racing devotees frequently indulge in the pointless exercise of comparing the merits of top performers from different generations but while that is a pleasant pastime for long winter evenings, it is not part of the terms of reference for this book. Therefore, we are content to admire some of the great champions of recent years without even trying to offer comparisons of ability.

Few better horses than the French-trained Sea Bird II have won the Derby during the post-war era. Racing in the colours of M. Jean Ternynck and ridden with supreme confidence by the Australian T. P. Glennon, Sea Bird II turned the 1965 Derby into a triumphant procession, never coming off the bit for a single stride in beating the subsequent Irish Derby and King George winner Meadow Court by a facile two lengths. If Sea Bird II was not the best winner of an Epsom Classic in living memory he was unquestionably the easiest.

Five years later came Nijinsky, trained for the American precious metals magnate Charles Engelhard by Vincent O'Brien, and one of Lester Piggott's record nine Derby winners. Having also won the 2,000 Guineas, Nijinsky was to complete the Triple Crown in the St Leger, the last colt to do so to date. This handsome son of the fabled Canadian stallion Northern Dancer, himself to become a notable Kentucky-based stallion, was rated by Piggott as 'just about the best horse I rode', which is a compliment indeed. Piggott certainly rode him with supreme confidence at Epsom, knowing the horse's startling acceleration could be applied whenever he chose.

Nijinsky, however, failed in his bid to land the Prix de l'Arc de Triomphe at the conclusion of a hectic season but his immediate successor on the list of Derby heroes, the pony-sized Mill Reef, was able to add the great Longchamp race

to his Derby laurels. Mill Reef's ability far outweighed his stature and his silk-smooth action can rarely have been bettered.

The Minstrel (1977) was another O'Brien–Piggott success story. He lacked the sheer class of Nijinsky or, indeed, the same trainer–jockey combination's Sir Ivor (1968) but was a colt of exemplary courage of whom owner Robert Sangster was rightly proud.

Shergar, the 10-length 1981 winner, so sadly to fall victim to kidnap and murder while at the Aga Khan's stud in Ireland, was the outstanding Derby winner of the past decade but perhaps the

A champion in repose. Brigadier Gerard at the Edgerton Stud, Newmarket 1981. Brigadier Gerard, winner of all but one of his races in a brilliant career, died in 1989.

best horse of the 1980s did not finish first in the Derby at all. Dancing Brave was beaten half a length in 1986 by Shahrastani, also owned by the Aga Khan, and must rank as the unluckiest Classic loser of modern times. After being held up by Greville Starkey, he could not get a clear run; when he at last saw daylight, Dancing Brave's finishing burst was breathtaking, but just too late. He proved subsequently to be greatly superior to Shahrastani but suffered from a hesitant and under-ambitious ride in the big race. Magnificent victories in the Eclipse Stakes, the King George VI and Queen Elizabeth

Diamond Stakes and the Arc de Triomphe illustrated the true worth of Khalid Abdullah's splendid champion.

During the same period the French-trained La Lagune (1968), Sun Princess, the 12-length winner in 1983, Oh So Sharp (1985) and Diminuendo (1988) were probably the pick of Oaks winners. Oh So Sharp may well have been the best of them and was certainly the most versatile, her Oaks success being the second stage in a fillies' Triple Crown initiated by a last-gasp win in the 1,000 Guineas and completed by an equally hard-fought success in the St Leger.

The 1989 season produced two high-quality colts in the middle-distance range, Nashwan and Old Vic, the former racing for Sheikh Hamdan Al-Maktoum and the latter for his younger brother Sheikh Mohammed. Between them they captured all three prime European versions of the Derby, Nashwan landing the Ever Ready Derby at Epsom and Old Vic both the French Derby, the Prix du Jockey-Club Lancia at Chantilly, and the Budweiser Irish Derby at the Curragh. All summer long, racing fans had hoped for a clash between them in Europe's championship event, the Ciga Prix de l'Arc de Triomphe, but in the end neither made it to Paris in the misty reaches of autumn.

Nashwan's splendid unbeaten run, which had included the 2,000 Guineas, Eclipse Stakes and the King George VI and Queen Elizabeth Diamond Stakes in addition to the Derby, came to an unexpected end in his Arc trial, the Prix Niel at Longchamp; meanwhile, Old Vic, having suffered a mid-season injury, had not regained full fitness in time to compete.

Retired to Sheikh Hamdan's Nunnery Stud in Norfolk to stand alongside his elder half-brother Unfuwain, Nashwan's great reputation had been dented slightly by his failure to remain undefeated but a syndication deal valued the big chestnut colt at £18 million and he should prove a fine stallion. Old Vic remained in training for 1990 with all the major mile and a half races on his shopping list.

It is unusual, in modern times, for a colt to win both the 2,000 Guineas and the Derby—

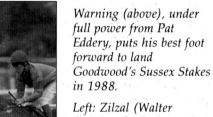

Warning (above), under full power from Pat Eddery, puts his best foot forward to land Goodwood's Sussex Stakes in 1988.

Left: Zilzal (Walter Swinburn) en route to victory in the 1989 Queen Elizabeth II Stakes at Ascot.

Below left: Don't Forget Me and Willie Carson win the 1987 General Accident 2,000 Guineas from Bellotto (Pat Eddery).

Above left: Nureyev (Philippe Paquet) pictured on 2,000 Guineas day in 1980. The French colt was first to pass the post but was disqualified in favour of Known Fact.

Top left: Robert Collet's Last Tycoon (Yves Saint-Martin) makes a successful cross-channel raid to land the 1986 William Hill Sprint Championship at York.

Centre left: Shadeed keeps on to master Bairn in the 1985 2,000 Guineas. Shadeed was Lester Piggott's 29th and last Classic winner.

Bottom left: The near-black Chief Singer stretches under Ray Cochrane to beat Never So Bold in the 1984 July Cup. The runner-up returned to take the Cup the following season.

213

Nashwan was the first to do so since Nijinsky in 1970—and for the fillies the 1,000 Guineas and Oaks double is just as hard to achieve. Musical Bliss, the 1989 1,000 Guineas heroine, made the attempt but failed to stay at Epsom, trailing home seventh behind the Aga Khan's lightly-raced Aliysa, her stablemate in the Michael Stoute yard at Newmarket. Walter Swinburn, Stoute's contract jockey, made the right choice of mount, leaving the South African Michael Roberts to partner Musical Bliss.

Of the specialist milers among the fillies during recent years, French stables seem to have produced a disproportionate number, headed by Miesque and Ravinella, respective winners of the 1,000 Guineas in 1987 and 1988. Miesque, who, like Ravinella, also captured the French Guineas (the Poule d'Essai des Pouliches) of her year, went on to become perhaps the outstanding miler of her sex during the post-war era, taking the $2 million Breeders' Cup Mile in the United States for two successive years. Her partnership with that fine French jockey Freddie Head provided one of the highlights of European racing during the 1980s, a period which saw many fine horses in action this side of the Atlantic.

The French have proved far more versatile than the British when raiding the multi-thousand dollar prizes in America, earning a much-feared reputation in the Breeders' Cup series and other important United States targets. Quite why this is the case is a matter for argument, but the answer may be that British owners and trainers woke up to the opportunities of winning these valuable races rather later in the day than their Gallic counterparts and so gave the French a head start. British racing as a whole has tended to remain somewhat insular while the boom has developed internationally, although there have been a number of honourable exceptions as discussed in the chapter on trainers. But now there are more and more British challenges for the great overseas prizes which, with meticulous planning, thorough preparation and, of course,

Right: Known Fact and Willie Carson (near side) just get the better of Kris and Joe Mercer to land the 1980 Queen Elizabeth II Stakes at Ascot.

Below right: Lucky No. 13 – Oh So Sharp snatches a last-stride success under Steve Cauthen in the 1985 1,000 Guineas. She went on to win the fillies' Triple Crown with victories in the Oaks and St Leger.

A moment of racing history as Willie Carson steers Troy (below) to an easy victory in the 1979 Derby, the 200th running of the world's most celebrated horse race.

Right: Pebbles, partnered by Pat Eddery, turns the 1985 Dubai Champion Stakes into a procession.

Sun Princess (below) receives a grateful pat from Willie Carson after carrying him to victory in the 1983 Oaks.

Diminuendo (below right), sailing home under Steve Cauthen to win the 1988 Gold Seal Oaks.

Bottom right: The splendid grey filly Indian Skimmer (Steve Cauthen), gaining one of her many victories in the 1987 Musidora Stakes at York.

Miesque (above), perhaps the best French-trained miler of the post-war era, races into the lead under Freddie Head to capture the 1987 General Accident 1,000 Guineas.

Left: Clive Brittain and his outstanding filly Pebbles, whose notable victories included the 1984 1,000 Guineas and the following season's Breeders' Cup Turf.

Top: Legal Case (Ray Cochrane) finishes fast on the far side to pip Dolpour (part hidden), Ile de Chypre and Scenic in the 1989 Dubai Champion Stakes.

Above: Walter Swinburn prepares to celebrate the 1989 General Accident 1,000 Guineas success of his mount Musical Bliss.

Above right: Scenic and Michael Hills (nearer camera) in a dead heat with Prince of Dance (Willie Carson) for the 1988 Dewhurst Stakes at Newmarket.

Above, far right: Mtoto (Michael Roberts) comes just too late to catch Italy's Tony Bin in a driving finish to the 1988 Prix de l'Arc de Triomphe. John Reid partnered the winner.

Extreme right: A mounted escort for Old Vic and Steve Cauthen following their triumph in the 1989 Budweiser Irish Derby at the Curragh.

Another Classic triumph for Pat Eddery, this time riding Hours After in the 1988 Prix du Jockey-Club Lancia at Chantilly (bottom right).

Right: Shahrastani and Walter Swinburn win the 1986 Ever Ready Derby from Dancing Brave (left). Dancing Brave was the unluckiest Derby loser in living memory.

Previous page: German-trained Star Appeal wins the 1975 Prix de l'Arc de Triomphe for jockey Greville Starkey watched by a huge Longchamp crowd and two apparently indifferent policemen.

Left: Dead Certain and Cash Asmussen flash past the winning post ahead of the pack in the 1989 Tattersalls Cheveley Park Stakes at Newmarket.

Below left: A surprise outcome to the 1989 Juddmonte International at York with Ile de Chypre (Tony Clark) beating his better-fancied stablemate Cacoethes (Greville Starkey).

the right equine 'ammunition' can certainly pay lucrative dividends.

Timing is arguably among the most important elements in racing but, despite the intricacies of the Pattern system, the European season is uneven with many of the most important races already staged by mid-summer. It is virtually impossible to keep any horse in prime racing condition from spring to late autumn so trainers with such targets as the English, French and Irish Derbys in mind, or the equivalent fillies' races, are likely to find their horses' form beginning to deteriorate when the October and November events such as the Arc de Triomphe and the Breeders' Cup are on the horizon.

For this reason neither the great French championship race nor the Breeders' Cup events necessarily result in the season's top horses winning, or even entering. A study of past results of the Arc de Triomphe, in particular, shows that it has become desirable, if not absolutely necessary, to adopt a quite different approach in order to have the best chance of landing this fabulous late-season spectacular. The approved method is to produce runners who have been rested since early summer with the exception of a single preparatory trial race within about a month of Arc day. The leading French trainers have this ploy down to a fine art and this helps explain why only a handful of horses from English stables have succeeded in capturing the Arc over a 30-year period. Going to Paris in the autumn, with the likelihood of soft ground, after a whole season of endeavour in the highest class of race, is clearly no recipe for victory.

It is possible for an exceptional horse to win both a Derby and an Arc de Triomphe. Mill Reef, the brilliant little champion of 1971, underlined that fact. But the list of Derby winners who failed to add the Arc to their major successes is depressingly long and serves to emphasize the problem faced by trainers who attempt a grand slam of the top European prizes in a single season. It seems connections must make an early choice between the great high-summer races and those end-of-season targets to stand a realistic chance of success. Only the greatest of horses can survive with their form intact throughout a racing year which might begin as early as March with preparation for one of the Guineas races, take in the Derby and the 'King George' and culminate with an attempt at the Arc de Triomphe or even the Breeders' Cup, run after the conclusion of the domestic season in early November. Those experts who claim that there is simply too much racing may have a sound point.

BIBLIOGRAPHY

British Racecourses by B. W. R. Curling (H. F. and G. Witherby Ltd).
Headquarters by Richard Onslow (Great Ouse Press).
Royal Ascot by Dorothy Laird (Hodder and Stoughton).
Goodwood by David Hunn (Davis-Poynter).
Horse Racing, the Inside Story by Noel Blunt (Hamlyn).
The Complete Book of the Horse by Pamela Macgregor-Morris (Book Club Associates).
Biographical Encyclopaedia of British Flat Racing by Roger Mortimer, Richard Onslow and Peter Willett (Macdonald and Janes).

1,000 GUINEAS STAKES

3-y-o fillies   Newmarket   1m

		Owner	Trainer	Jockey	SP
1946	HYPERICUM	HM King George	C. B.-Rochfort	D. Smith	100–6
1947	IMPRUDENCE	Mme P. Corbiere	J. Lieux	W. Johnstone	4–1
1948	QUEENPOT	Sir P. Loraine	N. Murless	G. Richards	6–1
1949	MUSIDORA	N. P. Donaldson	C. Elsey	E. Britt	100–8
1950	CAMAREE	J. Ternynck	A. Lieux	W. Johnstone	10–1
1951	BELLE OF ALL	R. S. Tufton	N. Bertie	G. Richards	4–1
1952	ZABARA	Sir M. McAlpine	V. Smyth	K. Gethin	7–1
1953	HAPPY LAUGHTER	H. D. H. Wills	J. Jarvis	E. Mercer	10–1
1954	FESTOON	J. A. Dewar	N. Cannon	A. Breasley	9–2
1955	MELD	Lady Z. Wernher	C. B.-Rochfort	W. Carr	11–4
1956	HONEYLIGHT	Sir V. Sassoon	C. Elsey	E. Britt	100–6
1957	ROSE ROYALE	HH Aga Khan	A. Head	C. Smirke	6–1
1958	BELLA PAOLA	M. F. Dupre	F. Mathet	S. Boullenger	8–11
1959	PETITE ETOILE	Prince Aly Khan	N. Murless	D. Smith	8–1
1960	NEVER TOO LATE	Mrs H. E. Jackson	E. Pollet	R. Poincelet	8–11
1961	SWEET SOLERA	Mrs S. M. Castello	R. Day	W. Rickaby	4–1
1962	ABERMAID	R. More O'Ferrall	H. Wragg	W. Williamson	100–6
1963	HULA DANCER	Mrs P. A. B. Widener	E. Pollet	R. Poincelet	1–2
1964	POURPARLER	Beatrice, Lady Granard	P. J. Prendergast	G. Bougoure	11–2
1965	NIGHT OFF	Major L. B. Holliday	W. Wharton	W. Williamson	9–2
1966	GLAD RAGS	Mrs J. P. Mills	M. V. O'Brien	P. Cook	100–6
1967	FLEET	R. C. Boucher	N. Murless	G. Moore	11–2
1968	CAERGWRIE	Mrs N. Murless	M. Murless	A. Barclay	4–1
1969	FULL DRESS II	R. B. Moller	H. Wragg	R. Hutchinson	7–1
1970	HUMBLE DUTY	Jean, Lady Ashcombe	P. Walwyn	L. Piggott	3–1
1971	ALTESSE ROYALE	F. R. Hue-Williams	N. Murless	Y. Saint-Martin	25–1
1972	WATERLOO	Mrs R. Stanley	J. W. Watts	E. Hide	8–1
1973	MYSTERIOUS	G. Pope Jr	N. Murless	G. Lewis	11–1
1974	HIGHCLERE	HM The Queen	W. Hern	J. Mercer	12–1
1975	NOCTURNAL SPREE	Mrs D. O'Kelly	H. V. S. Murless	J. Roe	14–1
1976	FLYING WATER	D. Wildenstein	A. Penna	Y. Saint-Martin	2–1
1977	MRS McARDY	Mrs E. Kettlewell	M. W. Easterby	E. Hide	16–1
1978	ENSTONE SPARK	R. Bonnycastle	B. Hills	E. Johnson	35–1
1979	ONE IN A MILLION	Helena Springfield Ltd	H. Cecil	J. Mercer	Evens
1980	QUICK AS LIGHTNING	O. Phipps	J. Dunlop	B. Rouse	12–1
1981	FAIRY FOOTSTEPS	H. J. Joel	H. Cecil	L. Piggott	6–4
1982	ON THE HOUSE	Sir P. Oppenheimer	H. Wragg	J. Reid	33–1
1983	MA BICHE	Sheikh Maktoum Al-Maktoum	Mme C. Head	F. Head	5–2
1984	PEBBLES	Capt. M. Lemos	C. Brittain	P. Robinson	8–1
1985	OH SO SHARP	Sheikh Mohammed Al-Maktoum	H. Cecil	S. Cauthen	2–1
1986	MIDWAY LADY	H. Ranier	B. Hanbury	R. Cochrane	10–1
1987	MIESQUE	S. Niarchos	F. Boutin	F. Head	15–8
1988	RAVINELLA	Ecurie Aland	Mme C. Head	G. W. Moore	4–5
1989	MUSICAL BLISS	Sheikh Mohammed Al-Maktoum	M. Stoute	W. R. Swinburn	7–2

2,000 GUINEAS STAKES

3-y-o   Newmarket   1m

		Owner	Trainer	Jockey	SP
1946	HAPPY KNIGHT	Sir W. Cooke	H. Jelliss	T. Weston	28–1
1947	TUDOR MINSTREL	J. A. Dewar	F. Darling	G. Richards	11–8
1948	MY BABU	HH Maharanee of Baroda	F. Armstrong	C. Smirke	2–1

Lester Piggott's ninth and final Derby triumph came on Teenoso in 1983.

1949	**NIMBUS**	Mrs M. Glenister	G. Colling	E.C. Elliott	10–1
1950	**PALESTINE**	HH Aga Khan	M. Marsh	C. Smirke	4–1
1951	**KI MING**	Ley On	M. Beary	A. Breasley	100–8
1952	**THUNDERHEAD II**	E. Constant	E. Pollet	R. Poincelet	100–7
1953	**NEARULA**	W. Humble	C. Elsey	E. Britt	2–1
1954	**DARIUS**	Sir P. Loraine	H. Wragg	E. Mercer	8–1
1955	**OUR BABU**	D. Robinson	G. Brooke	D. Smith	13–2
1956	**GILLES DE RETZ**	A. G. Samuel	C. Jerdein	F. Barlow	50–1
1957	**CREPELLO**	Sir V. Sassoon	N. Murless	L. Piggott	7–2
1958	**PALL MALL**	HM The Queen	C. B.-Rochfort	D. Smith	20–1
1959	**TABOUN**	Prince Aly Khan	A. Head	G. Moore	5–2
1960	**MARTIAL**	R. N. Webster	P. J. Prendergast	R. Hutchinson	18–1
1961	**ROCKAVON**	T. C. Yuill	G. Boyd	N. Stirk	66–1
1962	**PRIVY COUNCILLOR**	Major G. Glover	T. Waugh	W. Rickaby	100–6
1963	**ONLY FOR LIFE**	Miss M. Sheriffe	J. Tree	J. Lindley	33–1
1964	**BALDRIC II**	Mrs H. E. Jackson	E. Fellows	W. Pyers	20–1
1965	**NIKSAR**	W. Harvey	W. Nightingall	D. Keith	100–8
1966	**KASHMIR II**	Peter Butler	C. Bartholomew	J. Lindley	7–1
1967	**ROYAL PALACE**	H. J. Joel	N. Murless	G. Moore	100–30
1968	**SIR IVOR**	R. R. Guest	M. V. O'Brien	L. Piggott	11–8
1969	**RIGHT TACK**	J. R. Brown	J. Sutcliffe Jr	G. Lewis	15–2
1970	**NIJINSKY**	C. W. Engelhard	M. V. O'Brien	L. Piggott	4–7
1971	**BRIGADIER GERARD**	Mrs J. L. Hislop	W. Hern	J. Mercer	11–2
1972	**HIGH TOP**	Sir J. Thorn	B. van Cutsem	W. Carson	85–40

1973	**MON FILS**	Mrs B. Davis	R. Hannon	F. Durr	50–1
1974	**NONOALCO**	Mme M. Berger	F. Boutin	Y. Saint-Martin	19–2
1975	**BOLKONSKI**	C. d'Alessio	H. Cecil	G. Dettori	33–1
1976	**WOLLOW**	C. d'Alessio	H. Cecil	G. Dettori	Evens
1977	**NEBBIOLO**	N. Schibbye	K. Prendergast	G. Curran	20–1
1978	**ROLAND GARDENS**	J. Hayter	D. Sasse	F. Durr	28–1
1979	**TAP ON WOOD**	A. Shead	B. Hills	S. Cauthen	20–1
1980	**KNOWN FACT**	K. Abdulla	J. Tree	W. Carson	14–1
1981	**TO-AGORI-MOU**	Mrs A. Muinos	G. Harwood	G. Starkey	5–2
1982	**ZINO**	G. Oldham	F. Boutin	F. Head	8–1
1983	**LOMOND**	R. Sangster	M. V. O'Brien	P. Eddery	9–1
1984	**EL GRAN SENOR**	R. Sangster	M. V. O'Brien	P. Eddery	15–8
1985	**SHADEED**	Sheikh Maktoum Al-Maktoum	M. Stoute	L. Piggott	4–5
1986	**DANCING BRAVE**	K. Abdulla	G. Harwood	G. Starkey	15–8
1987	**DON'T FORGET ME**	J. Horgan	R. Hannon	W. Carson	9–1
1988	**DOYOUN**	HH Aga Khan	M. Stoute	W. R. Swinburn	4–5
1989	**NASHWAN**	Sheikh Hamdan Al-Maktoum	W. Hern	W. Carson	3–1

DERBY STAKES

3-y-o   Epsom   1m

		Owner	Trainer	Jockey	SP
1946	**AIRBORNE**	J. E. Ferguson	R. Perryman	T. Lowrey	50–1
1947	**PEARL DIVER**	Baron G. de Waldner	C. Halsey	G. Bridgland	40–1
1948	**MY LOVE**	HH Aga Khan	R. Carver	W. Johnstone	100–9
1949	**NIMBUS**	Mrs M. Glenister	G. Colling	E. C. Elliott	7–1
1950	**GALCADOR**	M. M. Boussac	C. Semblat	W. Johnstone	100–9
1951	**ARCTIC PRINCE**	J. McGrath	W. Stephenson	C. Spares	28–1
1952	**TULYAR**	HH Aga Khan	M. Marsh	C. Smirke	11–2
1953	**PINZA**	Sir V. Sassoon	N. Bertie	G. Richards	5–1
1954	**NEVER SAY DIE**	R. S. Clark	J. Lawson	L. Piggott	33–1
1955	**PHIL DRAKE**	Mme L. Volterra	F. Mathet	F. Palmer	100–8
1956	**LAVANDIN**	M. P. Wertheimer	A. Head	W. Johnstone	7–1
1957	**CREPELLO**	Sir V. Sassoon	N. Murless	L. Piggott	6–4
1958	**HARD RIDDEN**	Sir V. Sassoon	J. Rogers	C. Smirke	18–1
1959	**PARTHIA**	Sir H. de Trafford	C. B.-Rochfort	W. Carr	10–1
1960	**ST PADDY**	Sir V. Sassoon	N. Murless	L. Piggott	7–1
1961	**PSIDIUM**	Mrs A. Plesch	H. Wragg	R. Poincelet	66–1
1962	**LARKSPUR**	R. R. Guest	M. V. O'Brien	N. Sellwood	22–1
1963	**RELKO**	M. F. Dupre	F. Mathet	Y. Saint-Martin	5–1
1964	**SANTA CLAUS**	J. Ismay	J. Rogers	A. Breasley	15–8
1965	**SEA BIRD II**	J. Ternynck	E. Pollet	T. P. Glennon	7–4
1966	**CHARLOTTOWN**	Lady Z. Wernher	G. Smyth	A. Breasley	5–1
1967	**ROYAL PALACE**	H. J. Joel	N. Murless	G. Moore	7–4
1968	**SIR IVOR**	R. R. Guest	M. V. O'Brien	L. Piggott	4–5
1969	**BLAKENEY**	A. Budgett	A. Budgett	E. Johnson	15–2
1970	**NIJINSKY**	C. W. Engelhard	M. V. O'Brien	L. Piggott	11–8
1971	**MILL REEF**	P. Mellon	I. Balding	G. Lewis	100–30
1972	**ROBERTO**	J. W. Galbreath	M. V. O'Brien	L. Piggott	3–1
1973	**MORSTON**	A. Budgett	A. Budgett	E. Hide	25–1
1974	**SNOW KNIGHT**	Mrs N. Phillips	P. Nelson	B. Taylor	50–1
1975	**GRUNDY**	Dr C. Vittadini	P. Walwyn	P. Eddery	5–1
1976	**EMPERY**	N. B. Hunt	M. Zilber	L. Piggott	10–1
1977	**THE MINSTREL**	R. Sangster	M. V. O'Brien	L. Piggott	5–1
1978	**SHIRLEY HEIGHTS**	Lord Halifax	J. Dunlop	G. Starkey	8–1
1979	**TROY**	Sir M. Sobell	W. Hern	W. Carson	6–1
1980	**HENBIT**	Mrs A. Plesch	W. Hern	W. Carson	7–1
1981	**SHERGAR**	HH Aga Khan	M. Stoute	W. R. Swinburn	10–11
1982	**GOLDEN FLEECE**	R. Sangster	M. V. O'Brien	P. Eddery	3–1
1983	**TEENOSO**	E. Moller	G. Wragg	L. Piggott	9–2
1984	**SECRETO**	L. Miglietti	D. O'Brien	C. Roche	14–1
1985	**SLIP ANCHOR**	Lord H. de Walden	H. Cecil	S. Cauthen	9–4
1986	**SHAHRASTANI**	HH Aga Khan	M. Stoute	W. R. Swinburn	11–2
1987	**REFERENCE POINT**	L. Freedman	H. Cecil	S. Cauthen	6–4
1988	**KAHYASI**	HH Aga Khan	L. Cumani	R. Cochrane	11–1
1989	**NASHWAN**	Sheikh Hamdan Al-Maktoum	W. Hern	W. Carson	5–4

The perfect poise of a champion – Pat Eddery, who won the riding title for the seventh time in 1989.

OAKS STAKES

3-y-o fillies   Epsom   1m 4f

		Owner	Trainer	Jockey	SP
1946	STEADY AIM	Sir A. Butt	F. Butters	H. Wragg	7-1
1947	IMPRUDENCE	Mme P. Corbiere	J. Lieux	W. Johnstone	7-4
1948	MASAKA	HH Aga Khan	F. Butters	W. Nevett	7-1
1949	MUSIDORA	N. P. Donaldson	C. Elsey	E. Britt	4-1
1950	ASMENA	M. M. Boussac	C. Semblat	W. Johnstone	5-1
1951	NEASHAM BELLE	Major L. B. Holliday	G. Brooke	S. Clayton	33-1
1952	FRIEZE	Captain A. M. Keith	C. Elsey	E. Britt	100-7
1953	AMBIGUITY	Lord Astor	R. J. Colling	J. Mercer	18-1
1954	SUN CAP	Mme R. Forget	R. Carver	W. Johnstone	100-8
1955	MELD	Lady Z. Wernher	C. B.-Rochfort	W. Carr	7-4
1956	SICARELLE	Mme L. Volterra	F. Mathet	F. Palmer	3-1
1957	CARROZZA	HM The Queen	N. Murless	L. Piggott	100-8
1958	BELLA PAOLA	M. F. Dupre	F. Mathet	M. Garcia	6-4
1959	PETITE ETOILE	Prince Aly Khan	N. Murless	L. Piggott	11-2
1960	NEVER TOO LATE	H. E. Jackson	E. Pollet	R. Poincelet	6-5
1961	SWEET SOLERA	Mrs S. M. Castello	F. Day	W. Rickaby	11-4
1962	MONADE	G. P. Goulandris	J. Lieux	Y. Saint-Martin	7-1
1963	NOBLESSE	Mrs J. M. Olin	P. J. Prendergast	G. Bougoure	4-11
1964	HOMEWARD BOUND	Sir F. Robinson	J. Oxley	G. Starkey	100-7
1965	LONG LOOK	J. Cox Brady	M. V. O'Brien	J. Purtell	100-7
1966	VALORIS	C. Clore	M. V. O'Brien	L. Piggott	11-10
1967	PIA	Countess M. Batthyany	W. Elsey	E. Hide	100-7
1968	LA LAGUNE	M. H. Berlin	F. Boutin	G. Thiboeuf	11-8
1969	SLEEPING PARTNER	Lord Rosebury	Doug Smith	J. Gorton	100-6
1970	LUPE	Mrs S. Joel	N. Murless	A. Barclay	100-30
1971	ALTESSE ROYALE	F. R. Hue-Williams	N. Murless	G. Lewis	6-4
1972	GINEVRA	C. A. B. St George	Ryan Price	A. Murray	8-1
1973	MYSTERIOUS	G. Pope Jr	N. Murless	G. Lewis	13-8
1974	POLYGAMY	L. Freedman	P. Walwyn	P. Eddery	3-1
1975	JULIETTE MARNY	J. Morrison	J. Tree	L. Piggott	12-1
1976	PAWNEESE	D. Wildenstein	A. Penna	Y. Saint-Martin	6-5
1977	DUNFERMLINE	HM The Queen	W. Hern	W. Carson	6-1
1978	FAIR SALINIA	S. Hanson	M. Stoute	G. Starkey	8-1
1979	SCINTILLATE	J. Morrison	J. Tree	P. Eddery	20-1
1980	BIREME	R. Hollingsworth	W. Hern	W. Carson	9-2
1981	BLUE WIND	Mrs B. Firestone	D. Weld	L. Piggott	3-1
1982	TIME CHARTER	R. Barnett	H. Candy	W. Newnes	12-1
1983	SUN PRINCESS	Sir M. Sobell	W. Hern	W. Carson	11-1
1984	CIRCUS PLUME	Sir R. McAlpine	J. Dunlop	L. Piggott	4-1
1985	OH SO SHARP	Sheikh Mohammed Al-Maktoum	H. Cecil	S. Cauthen	6-4
1986	MIDWAY LADY	H. Ranier	B. Hanbury	R. Cochrane	15-8
1987	UNITE	Sheikh Mohammed Al-Maktoum	M. Stoute	W. R. Swinburn	11-1
1988	DIMINUENDO	Sheikh Mohammed Al-Maktoum	H. Cecil	S. Cauthen	7-4
1989	ALIYSA	HH Aga Khan	M. Stoute	W. R. Swinburn	11-10

ST LEGER STAKES

3-y-o   Doncaster   1m 6f 132yds

		Owner	Trainer	Jockey	SP
1946	AIRBORNE	J. E. Ferguson	R. Perryman	T. Lowrey	3-1
1947	SAYAJIRAO	HH Maharanee of Baroda	F. Armstrong	E. Britt	9-2
1948	BLACK TARQUIN	W. Woodward	C. B.-Rochfort	E. Britt	15-2
1949	RIDGE WOOD	G. R. Smith	N. Murless	M. Beary	100-7
1950	SCRATCH II	M. M. Boussac	C. Semblat	W. Johnstone	9-2
1951	TALMA II	M. M. Boussac	C. Semblat	W. Johnstone	7-1
1952	TULYAR	HH Aga Khan	M. Marsh	C. Smirke	10-11
1953	PREMONITION	W. P. Wyatt	C. B.-Rochfort	E. Smith	10-1
1954	NEVER SAY DIE	R. S. Clark	J. Lawson	C. Smirke	100-30
1955	MELD	Lady Z. Wernher	C. B.-Rochfort	W. Carr	10-11
1956	CAMBREMER	R. B. Strassburger	C. Bridgland	F. Palmer	8-1
1957	BALLYMOSS	J. McShain	M. V. O'Brien	T. P. Burns	8-1
1958	ALCIDE	Sir H. de Trafford	C. B.-Rochfort	W. Carr	4-9
1959	CANTELO	W. Hill	C. Elsey	E. Hide	100-7
1960	ST PADDY	Sir V. Sassoon	N. Murless	L. Piggott	4-6

1961	**AURELIUS**	V. Lilley	N. Murless	L. Piggott	9–2
1962	**HETHERSETT**	Major L. B. Holliday	W. Hern	W. Carr	100–8
1963	**RAGUSA**	J. R. Mullion	P. J. Prendergast	G. Bougoure	2–5
1964	**INDIANA**	C. W. Engelhard	J. F. Watts	J. Lindley	100–7
1965	**PROVOKE**	J. J. Astor	W. Hern	J. Mercer	28–1
1966	**SODIUM**	R. J. Sigtia	G. Todd	F. Durr	7–1
1967	**RIBOCCO**	C. W. Engelhard	R. Johnson Houghton	L. Piggott	7–2
1968	**RIBERO**	C. W. Engelhard	R. Johnson Houghton	L. Piggott	100–30
1969	**INTERMEZZO**	G. A. Oldham	H. Wragg	R. Hutchinson	7–1
1970	**NIJINSKY**	C. W. Engelhard	M. V. O'Brien	L. Piggott	2–7
1971	**ATHENS WOOD**	Mrs J. Rogerson	H. Thomson Jones	L. Piggott	5–2
1972	**BOUCHER**	O. Phipps	M. V. O'Brien	L. Piggott	3–1
1973	**PELEID**	Colonel W. Behrens	W. Elsey	F. Durr	28–1
1974	**BUSTINO**	Lady Beaverbrook	W. Hern	J. Mercer	11–10
1975	**BRUNI**	C. A. B. St George	Ryan Price	A. Murray	9–1
1976	**CROW**	D. Wildenstein	A. Penna	Y. Saint-Martin	6–1
1977	**DUNFERMLINE**	HM The Queen	W. Hern	W. Carson	10–1
1978	**JULIO MARINER**	M. Lemos	C. Brittain	E. Hide	28–1
1979	**SON OF LOVE**	A. Rolland	R. Collett	A. Lequeux	20–1
1980	**LIGHT CAVALRY**	H. J. Joel	H. Cecil	J. Mercer	3–1
1981	**CUT ABOVE**	Sir J. Astor	W. Hern	J. Mercer	28–1
1982	**TOUCHING WOOD**	Sheikh Maktoum Al-Maktoum	H. Thomson Jones	P. Cook	7–1
1983	**SUN PRINCESS**	Sir M. Sobell	W. Hern	W. Carson	11–8
1984	**COMMANCHE RUN**	I. Allan	L. Cumani	L. Piggott	7–4
1985	**OH SO SHARP**	Sheikh Mohammed Al-Maktoum	H. Cecil	S. Cauthen	8–11
1986	**MOON MADNESS**	Lavinia Duchess of Norfolk	J. Dunlop	P. Eddery	9–2
1987	**REFERENCE POINT**	L. Freedman	H. Cecil	S. Cauthen	4–11
1988	**MINSTER SON**	Dowager Lady Beaverbrook	N. Graham	W. Carson	15–2
*1989	**MICHELOZZO**	C. A. B. St George	H. Cecil	S. Cauthen	6–4

*Run at Ayr.

IRISH 1,000 GUINEAS

The Curragh   1m

		Owner	**Trainer**	**Jockey**	**SP**
1960	**ZENOBIA**	Mrs A. Biddle	T. Shaw	L. Ward	100–8
1961	**LADY SENATOR**	G. Freeman	P. Ashworth	T. Gosling	6–4
1962	**SHANDON BELLE**	S. Abbot	R. Fetherstonhaugh	T. P. Burns	20–1
1963	**GAZPACHO**	Mrs J. Mullion	P. J. Prendergast	F. Palmer	9–1
1964	**ROYAL DANSEUSE**	J. McGrath	S. McGrath	J. Roe	7–4
1965	**ARDENT DANCER**	Mrs P. McAllister	T. Gosling	W. Rickaby	5–1
1966	**VALORIS**	C. Clore	M. V. O'Brien	J. Power	9–1
1967	**LACQUER**	R. Moller	H. Wragg	R. Hutchinson	4–1
1968	**FRONT ROW**	F. Allen	R. Jarvis	E. Eldin	7–1
1969	**WENDUYNE**	J. Mullion	P. J. Prendergast	W. Williamson	2–1
1970	**BLACK SATIN**	W. Reynolds	J. Dunlop	R. Hutchinson	3–1
1971	**FAVOLETTA**	R. Moller	H. Wragg	L. Piggott	5–2
1972	**PIDGET**	N. Butler	K. Prendergast	W. Swinburn	20–1
1973	**CLOONAGH**	A. B.-Rochfort	H. Cecil	G. Starkey	7–1
1974	**GAILY**	Sir M. Sobell	W. Hern	R. Hutchinson	11–5
1975	**MIRALLA**	Lady Lister Kaye	Sir H. Nugent	R. F. Parnell	14–1
1976	**SARAH SIDDONS**	Mrs J. Mullion	P. J. Prendergast	G. Roche	9–2
1977	**LADY CAPULET**	R. Sangster	M. V. O'Brien	T. Murphy	16–1
1978	**MORE SO**	L. Gelb	P. J. Prendergast	C. Roche	2–1
1979	**GODETIA**	R. Sangster	M. V. O'Brien	L. Piggott	4–6
1980	**CAIRN ROUGE**	D. Brady	M. Cunningham	A. Murray	5–1
1981	**ARCTIQUE ROYALE**	J. P. Binet	K. Prendergast	G. Curran	7–1
1982	**PRINCE'S POLLY**	K. Fitzpatrick	D. Weld	W. Swinburn	12–1
1983	**L'ATTRAYANTE**	Mme C. Thieriot	O. Douieb	A. Badel	4–1
1984	**KATIES**	T. Ramsden	M. Ryan	P. Robinson	20–1
1985	**AL BAHATHRI**	Sheikh Hamdan Al-Maktoum	H. Thomson-Jones	A. Murray	7–1
1986	**SONIC LADY**	Sheikh Mohammed Al-Maktoum	M. Stoute	W. R. Swinburn	4–1
1987	**FOREST FLOWER**	P. Mellon	I. Balding	T. Ives	4–1
1988	**TRUSTED PARTNER**	Moyglare Stud Farm	D. Weld	M. J. Kinane	10–1
1989	**ENSCONSE**	Sheikh Mohammed Al-Maktoum	L. Cumani	R. Cochrane	13–8

IRISH 2,000 GUINEAS

The Curragh   1m

		Owner	Trainer	Jockey	SP
1960	KYTHNOS	E. More O'Ferrall	P. J. Prendergast	R. Hutchinson	5–4
1961	LIGHT YEAR	T. Hallinan	A. O'Brien	G. Bougoure	6–1
1962	ARCTIC STORM	Mrs E. Carroll	J. Oxx	W. Williamson	20–1
1963	LINACRE	Lord Ennisdale	P. J. Prendergast	P. Matthews	40–1
1964	SANTA CLAUS	J. Ismay	J. Rogers	W. Burke	Evens
1965	GREEN BANNER	B. Kerr	K. Kerr	N. Brennan	100–7
1966	PAVEH	P. Widener	T. Ainsworth	T. P. Burns	9–1
1967	ATHERSTONE	S. O'Flaherty	S. Quirke	R. Parnell	100–7
1968	MISTIGO	F. Feeney	S. Quirke	R. Parnell	10–1
1969	RIGHT TACK	J. Brown	J. Sutcliffe	G. Lewis	Evens
1970	DECIES	N. B. Hunt	B. van Cutsem	L. Piggott	8–13
1971	KING'S COMPANY	B. Firestone	G. Robinson	F. Head	9–2
1972	BALLYMORE	Mrs J. Mullion	P. J. Prendergast	C. Roche	33–1
1973	SHARP EDGE	J. Astor	W. Hern	J. Mercer	5–2
1974	FURRY GLEN	P. McGrath	S. McGrath	G. McGrath	10–1
1975	GRUNDY	Dr C. Vittadini	P. Walwyn	P. Eddery	10–11
1976	NORTHERN TREASURE	A. Brennan	K. Prendergast	G. Curran	33–1
1977	PAMPAPAUL	H. Paul	H. V. Murless	G. Dettori	16–1
1978	JAAZEIRO	R. Sangster	M. V. O'Brien	L. Piggott	11–4
1979	DICKINS HILL	Mme J. Binet	M. O'Toole	A. Murray	5–2
1980	NIKOLI	Lord Iveagh	P. J. Prendergast	C. Roche	5–1
1981	KING'S LAKE	J. P. Binet	M. V. O'Brien	P. Eddery	5–1
1982	DARA MONARCH	Mrs L. Browne	L. Browne	M. J. Kinane	20–1
1983	WASSL	Sheik Ahmed Al-Maktoum	J. Dunlop	A. Murray	12–1
1984	SADLERS WELLS	R. Sangster	M. V. O'Brien	G. McGrath	10–1
1985	TRIPTYCH	A. Clore	D. O'Brien	C. Roche	7–1
1986	FLASH OF STEEL	B. Firestone	D. Weld	M. Kinane	9–2
1987	DON'T FORGET ME	J. Horgan	R. Hannon	W. Carson	6–4
1988	PRINCE OF BIRDS	R. Sangster	M. V. O'Brien	D. Gillespie	9–1
1989	SHAADI	Sheikh Mohammed Al-Maktoum	M. Stoute	W. R. Swinburn	7–2

It takes massive amounts of liquids and fodder to keep a racehorse fit for action and here Clive Brittain's Lapierre poses with stable feeder Mick Leaman (left) and his lad Phil Chambers, and a typical ration for just a single week. (See diagram).

LAPIERRE'S FEED PROGRAMME

1 Hay (Devon)
2 Sack of Australian Oats
3 Tub of Guinness
4 American Hay
5 Tub of chaff & lucerne
6 Comfrey leaves
7 Tub of mash (Wed & Sat only)
8 Wheat Germ Oil
9 Twydil pellets
10 Twydil Hemopar
11 21 eggs
12 Carrots
13 Molasses
14 Garlic Honey
15 Super E Glucose
16 Electrolytes
17 Salt
18 Sulphur

IRISH DERBY

The Curragh 1m 4f

		Owner	Trainer	Jockey	SP
1960	CHAMOUR	F. Burmann	A. O'Brien	G. Bougoure	3–1
1961	YOUR HIGHNESS	Mrs S. Joel	H. Cottrill	H. Holmes	33–1
1962	TAMBOURINE II	Mrs H. Jackson	E. Pollet	R. Poincelet	15–2
1963	RAGUSA	J. Mullion	P. J. Prendergast	G. Bougoure	100–7
1964	SANTA CLAUS	J. Ismay	J. Rogers	W. Burke	4–7
1965	MEADOW COURT	G. Bell	P. J. Prendergast	L. Piggott	11–10
1966	SODIUM	R. Sigtia	G. Todd	F. Durr	13–2
1967	RIBOCCO	C. Engelhard	R. Johnson Houghton	L. Piggott	5–2
1968	RIBERO	C. Engelhard	R. Johnson Houghton	L. Piggott	100–6
1969	PRINCE REGENT	Comte de la Valdene	E. Pollet	G. Lewis	7–2
1970	NIJINSKY	C. Engelhard	M. V. O'Brien	L. Ward	4–11
1971	IRISH BALL	E. Littler	P. Lallie	A. Gibert	7–2
1972	STEEL PULSE	R. Tikkoo	A. Breasley	W. Williamson	10–1
1973	WEAVER'S HALL	S. McGrath	S. McGrath	G. McGrath	33–1
1974	ENGLISH PRINCE	Mrs V. Hue-Williams	P. Walwyn	Y. Saint-Martin	8–1
1975	GRUNDY	Dr C. Vittadini	P. Walwyn	P. Eddery	9–10
1976	MALACATE	Mme M. Berger	F. Boutin	P. Paquet	5–1
1977	THE MINSTREL	R. Sangster	M. V. O'Brien	L. Piggott	11–10
1978	SHIRLEY HEIGHTS	Lord Halifax	J. Dunlop	G. Starkey	5–4
1979	TROY	Sir M. Sobell	W. Hern	W. Carson	4–9
1980	TYRNAVOS	G. Cambanis	B. Hobbs	A. Murray	25–1
1981	SHERGAR	HH Aga Khan	M. Stoute	L. Piggott	1–3
1982	ASSERT	R. Sangster	D. O'Brien	C. Roche	4–7
1983	SHAREEF DANCER	Sheik Maktoum Al-Maktoum	M. Stoute	W. R. Swinburn	8–1
1984	EL GRAN SENOR	R. Sangster	M. V. O'Brien	P. Eddery	2–7
1985	LAW SOCIETY	S. Niarchos	M. V. O'Brien	P. Eddery	15–8
1986	SHAHRASTANI	HH Aga Khan	M. Stoute	W. R. Swinburn	Evens
1987	SIR HARRY LEWIS	H. Kaskel	B. Hills	J. Reid	6–1
1988	KAHYASI	HH Aga Khan	L. Cumani	R. Cochrane	4–5
1989	OLD VIC	Sheikh Mohammed Al-Maktoum	H. Cecil	S. Cauthen	4–11

IRISH OAKS

The Curragh 1m 4f

		Owner	Trainer	Jockey	SP
1960	LYNCHRIS	Mrs E. Fawcett	J. Oxx	W. Williamson	11–4
1961	AMBERGRIS	R. More O'Ferrall	H. Wragg	J. Lindley	6–4
1962	FRENCH CREAM	R. Dennis	G. Brooke	W. Rickaby	100–9
1963	HIBERNIA III	Dr M. Andree	J. Oxx	W. Williamson	6–4
1964	ANCASTA	F. Burmann	M. V. O'Brien	J. Purtell	3–1
1965	AURABELLA	Lt-Col. J. Silcock	M. V. O'Brien	L. Ward	22–1
1966	MERRY MATE	J. McShain	J. Oxx	W. Williamson	100–9
1967	PAMPALINA	Mrs B. Aitken	J. Oxx	J. Roe	100–8
1968	CELINA	Mrs J. Hindley	N. Murless	A. Barclay	4–1
1969	GALA	Mrs J. Hanes	M. V. O'Brien	L. Ward	9–1
1970	SANTA TINA	S. O'Flaherty	C. Millbank	L. Piggott	5–2
1971	ALTESSE ROYALE	Colonel F. Hue-Williams	N. Murless	G. Lewis	1–2
1972	REGAL EXCEPTION	R. Scully	J. Fellows	M. Philipperon	4–1
1973	DAHLIA	N. B. Hunt	M. Zilber	W. Pyers	8–1
1974	DIBIDALE	N. Robinson	B. Hills	W. Carson	7–4
1975	JULIETTE MARNY	J. Morrison	J. Tree	L. Piggott	5–2
1976	LAGUNETTE	M. Berghracht	F. Boutin	P. Paquet	3–1
1977	OLWYN	S. Vanian	R. Boss	J. Lynch	11–1
1978	FAIR SALINIA	S. Hanson	M. Stoute	G. Starkey	3–1
1979	GODETIA	R. Sangster	M. V. O'Brien	L. Piggott	6–4
1980	SHOOT A LINE	R. Budgett	W. Hern	W. Carson	6–4
1981	BLUE WIND	Mrs B. Firestone	D. Weld	W. Swinburn	4–6
1982	SWIFTFOOT	Lord Rotherwick	W. Hern	W. Carson	4–1
1983	GIVE THANKS	Mrs O. White	J. Bolger	D. Gillespie	7–4
1984	PRINCESS PATI	Mrs J. Mullion	C. Collins	P. Shanahan	9–2
1985	HELEN STREET	Sir M. Sobell	W. Hern	W. Carson	3–1

1986	**COLORSPIN**	Helena Springfield Ltd	M. Stoute	P. Eddery	6-1
1987	**UNITE**	Sheikh Mohammed Al-Maktoum	M. Stoute	W. R. Swinburn	8-13
*1988	**DIMINUENDO**	Sheikh Mohammed Al-Maktoum	H. Cecil	S. Cauthen	2-9
	MELODIST	Sheikh Mohammed Al-Maktoum	M. Stoute	W. R. Swinburn	11-1
1989	**ALYDARESS**	Sheikh Mohammed Al-Maktoum	H. Cecil	M. J. Kinane	7-4

*1988 was a dead heat

IRISH ST LEGER

The Curragh   1m 6f

		Owner	Trainer	Jockey	SP
1960	**LYNCHRIS**	Mrs E. Fawcett	J. Oxx	W. Williamson	4-6
1961	**VIMADEE**	Mrs T. McCairns	T. Burns	T. P. Burns	100-9
1962	**ARCTIC VALE**	Mrs E. Goring	P. J. Prendergast	P. Matthews	40-1
1963	**CHRISTMAS ISLAND**	Lord Ennisdale	P. J. Prendergast	G. Bougoure	6-1
1964	**BISCAYNE**	Mrs J. Reid	J. Oxx	W. Williamson	4-1
1965	**CRAIGHOUSE**	Lord Astor	W. Hern	J. Mercer	6-1
1966	**WHITE GLOVES**	Mrs M. Moore	M. V. O'Brien	L. Ward	4-1
1967	**DAN KANO**	S. Raccah	J. Lenehan	L. Piggott	Evens
1968	**GIOLLA MEAR**	HE The President	M. Hurley	P. Berry	8-1
1969	**REINDEER**	R. Guest	M. V. O'Brien	L. Ward	5-2
1970	**ALLANGRANGE**	J. McGrath	S. McGrath	G. McGrath	9-1
1971	**PARNELL**	R. More O'Ferrall	S. Quirke	A. Simpson	11-5
1972	**PIDGET**	N. Butler	K. Prendergast	T. Burns	13-2
1973	**CONOR PASS**	Mrs R. More	K. Prendergast	P. Jarman	5-1
1974	**MISTIGRI**	E. More O'Ferrall	P. J. Prendergast	C. Roche	9-1
1975	**CAUCASUS**	Mrs C. Engelhard	M. V. O'Brien	L. Piggott	3-1
1976	**MENEVAL**	Mrs G. Getty II	M. V. O'Brien	L. Piggott	5-4
1977	**TRANSWORLD**	S. Fraser	M. V. O'Brien	T. Murphy	13-2
1978	**M-LOISHAN**	Essa Alkhalifa	H. R. Price	B. Taylor	2-1
1979	**NINISKI**	Lady Beaverbrook	W. Hern	W. Carson	11-10
1980	**GONZALES**	R. Sangster	M. V. O'Brien	R. Carroll	4-7
1981	**PROTECTION RACKET**	S. Fradkoff	J. Hindley	B. Taylor	6-4
1982	**TOUCHING WOOD**	Sheik Maktoum Al-Maktoum	H. Thomson Jones	P. Cook	5-4
1983	**MOUNTAIN LODGE**	Lord Halifax	J. Dunlop	D. Gillespie	13-2
1984	**OPALE**	Snailwell Stud Co.	A. Stewart	D. McHargue	11-4
1985	**LEADING COUNSEL**	R. Sangster	M. V. O'Brien	P. Eddery	7-4
1986	**AUTHAAL**	Sheikh Mohammed Al-Maktoum	D. O'Brien	C. Roche	8-1
1987	**EUROBIRD**	G. Jennings	J. Oxx	C. Asmussen	9-4
1988	**DARK LOMOND**	S. Niarchos	M. V. O'Brien	D. Gillespie	10-1
1989	**PETITE ILE**	J. F. Malle	J. Oxx	R. Quinton	3-1

POULE D'ESSAI DES POULAINS

Longchamp   1m

		Owner	Trainer	Jockey
1960	**MINCIO**	M. Lehmann	W. Head	F. Palmer
1961	**RIGHT ROYAL V**	Mme J. Couturie	E. Pollet	R. Poincelet
1962	**ADAMASTOR**	Mme A. Magnus	W. Head	Y. Saint-Martin
1963	**RELKO**	F. Dupre	F. Mathet	Y. Saint-Martin
1964	**NEPTUNUS**	Mme J. Couturie	E. Pollet	T. Glennon
1965	**CAMBREMONT**	J. Bouchara	W. Head	J. Massard
1966	**SOLEIL**	Baron G. de Rothschild	G. Watson	J. Deforge
1967	**BLUE TOM**	Mme P. Widener	E. Pollet	J. Deforge
1968	**ZEDDAAN**	HH Aga Khan	F. Mathet	Y. Saint-Martin
1969	**DON II**	M. Wildenstein	M. Zilber	W. Pyers
1970	**CARO**	Countess M. Batthyany	A. Klimscha	W. Williamson
1971	**ZUG**	W. Hawn	J. Cunnington	J. Desaint
1972	**RIVERMAN**	Mme P. Wertheimer	A. Head	J. Desaint
1973	**KALAMOUN**	HH Aga Khan	F. Mathet	H. Samani
1974	**MOULINES**	J. Kashiyama	R. Carver	M. Philipperon
1975	**GREEN DANCER**	J. Wertheimer	A. Head	F. Head
1976	**RED LORD**	J. Wertheimer	A. Head	F. Head
1977	**BLUSHING GROOM**	HH Aga Khan	F. Mathet	H. Samani
1978	**NISHAPOUR**	HH Aga Khan	F. Mathet	H. Samani
1979	**IRISH RIVER**	Mme R. Ades	J. Cunnington Jr	M. Philipperon
1980	**IN FIJAR**	M. Fustok	M. Saliba	G. Doleuze

1981	**RECITATION**	A. Bodie	G. Harwood	G. Starkey
1982	**MELYNO**	S. Niarchos	F. Mathet	Y. Saint-Martin.
1983	**L'EMIGRANT**	S. Niarchos	F. Boutin	C. Asmussen
1984	**SIBERIAN EXPRESS**	M. Fustok	A. Fabre	A. Gibert
1985	**NO PASS NO SALE**	R. Strauss	R. Collet	Y. Saint-Martin
1986	**FAST TOPAZE**	M. Fustok	G. Mikhalides	C. Asmussen
1987	**SOVIET STAR**	Sheikh Mohammed Al-Maktoum	A. Fabre	G. Starkey
1988	**BLUSHING JOHN**	A. Paulson	F. Boutin	F. Head
1989	**KENDOR**	A. Bader	R. Touflan	M. Philipperon

POULE D'ESSAI DES POULICHES

Longchamp   1m

		Owner	Trainer	Jockey
1960	**TIMANDRA**	Baron G. de Rothschild	G. Watson	G. Boulanger
1961	**SOLITUDE**	F. Dupre	F. Mathet	Y. Saint-Martin
1962	**LA SEGA**	F. Dupre	F. Mathet	Y. Saint-Martin
1963	**ALTISSIMA**	Mme N. Tuan	R. Pelat	R. Poincelet
1964	**RAJPUT PRINCESS**	G. Flipo	C. Bartholomew	L. Piggott
1965	**LA SARRE**	Mme R. Strassburger	L. Baldisseri	R. Poincelet
1966	**RIGHT AWAY**	Mme P. Widener	E. Pollet	A. Breasley
1967	**GAZALA**	N. B. Hunt	J. Cunnington Jr	H. Samani
1968	**POLA BELLA**	Mme F. Dupre	F. Mathet	Y. Saint-Martin
1969	**KOBLENZA**	Mme F. Dupre	F. Mathet	Y. Saint-Martin
1970	**PAMPERED MISS**	N. B. Hunt	J. Cunnington Jr	M. Philipperon
1971	**BOLD FASCINATOR**	W. Rosso	J. Fellows	W. Williamson
1972	**MATA HARI**	Countes M. Batthyany	A. Penna	J. Cruget
1973	**ALLEZ FRANCE**	D. Wildenstein	A. Klimscha	Y. Saint-Martin
1974	**DUMKA**	G. Bauer	J. de Chevigny	A. Lequeux
1975	**IVANJICA**	J. Wertheimer	A. Head	F. Head
1976	**RIVERQUEEN**	Mme A. Head	C. Datessen	F. Head
1977	**MADELIA**	D. Wildenstein	A. Penna	Y. Saint-Martin
1978	**DANCING MAID**	J. Wertheimer	A. Head	F. Head
1979	**THREE TROIKAS**	Mme A. Head	Mme C. Head	F. Head
1980	**ARYENNE**	D. Volkert	J. Fellows	M. Philipperon
1981	**UKRAINE GIRL**	Mrs J. Mullion	R. Collet	P. Eddery
1982	**RIVER LADY**	R. Sangster	F. Boutin	L. Piggott
1983	**L'ATTRAYANTE**	Mme C. Thieriot	O. Douieb	A. Badel
1984	**MASARIKA**	HH Aga Khan	A. de Royer-Dupre	Y. Saint-Martin
1985	**SILVERMINE**	Mme A. Head	Mme C. Head	F. Head
1986	**BAISER VOLE**	R. Sangster	Mme C. Head	G. Guignard
1987	**MIESQUE**	S. Niarchos	F. Boutin	F. Head
1988	**RAVINELLA**	Ecurie Aland	Mme C. Head	G. W. Moore
1989	**PEARL BRACELET**	Ecurie Fustok	R. Wojtowiez	A. Gibert

PRIX DU JOCKEY-CLUB

Chantilly   1m 4f

		Owner	Trainer	Jockey
1960	**CHARLOTTESVILLE**	HH Aga Khan	A. Head	G. Moore
1961	**RIGHT ROYAL V**	Mme J. Coururie	E. Pollet	R. Poincelet
1962	**VAL DE LOIR**	Marquise du Vivier	M. Bonaventure	F. Palmer
1963	**SANCTUS**	J. Ternynck	E. Pollet	M. Larraun
1964	**LE FABULEUX**	Mme G. Weisweiller	W. Head	J. Massard
1965	**RELIANCE II**	F. Dupre	F. Mathet	Y. Saint-Martin
1966	**NELCIUS**	M. Duboscq	M. Clement	Y. Saint-Martin
1967	**ASTEC**	Baron de la Rochette	A. Mieux	A. Jezequal
1968	**TAPALQUE**	A. Plesch	F. Mathet	Y. Saint-Martin
1969	**GOODLY**	M. Lehmann	W. Head	F. Head
1970	**SASSAFRAS**	A. Plesch	F. Mathet	Y. Saint-Martin
1971	**RHEFFIC**	F. Dupre	F. Mathet	W. Pyers
1972	**HARD TO BEAT**	J. Kashiyama	R. Carver	L. Piggott
1973	**ROI LEAR**	Mme P. Wertheimer	A. Head	F. Head
1974	**CARACOLERO**	Mme M.-F. Berger	F. Boutin	P. Paquet
1975	**VAL DE L'ORNE**	J. Wertheimer	A. Head	F. Head
1976	**YOUTH**	N. B. Hunt	M. Zilber	F. Head

1977	**CRYSTAL PALACE**	Baron G. de Rothschild	F. Mathet	G. Dubroeucq
1978	**ACAMAS**	M. Boussac	G. Bonaventure	Y. Saint-Martin
1979	**TOP VILLE**	HH Aga Khan	F. Mathet	Y. Saint-Martin
1980	**POLICEMAN**	F. Tinsley	C. Millbank	W. Carson
1981	**BIKALA**	J. Ouaki	P. L. Biancone	S. Gorli
1982	**ASSERT**	R. Sangster	D. O'Brien	C. Roche
1983	**CAERLEON**	R. Sangster	M. V. O'Brien	P. Eddery
1984	**DARSHAAN**	HH Aga Khan	A. de Royer-Dupre	Y. Saint-Martin
1985	**MOUKTAR**	HH Aga Khan	A. de Royer-Dupre	Y. Saint-Martin
1986	**BERING**	Mme A. Head	Mme C. Head	G. W. Moore
1987	**NATROUN**	HH Aga Khan	A. de Royer-Dupre	Y. Saint-Martin
1988	**HOURS AFTER**	Marquesa de Moratalla	P. L. Biancone	P. Eddery
1989	**OLD VIC**	Sheikh Mohammed Al-Maktoum	H. Cecil	S. Cauthen

PRIX DE DIANE

Chantilly   1m 2f 110yds

		Owner	**Trainer**	**Jockey**
1960	**TIMANDRA**	Baron G. de Rothschild	G. Watson	G. Boullenger
1961	**HERMIERES**	Baron G. de Rothschild	G. Watson	G. Boullenger
1962	**LE SEGA**	F. Dupre	F. Mathet	Y. Saint-Martin
1963	**BELLE FERRONIERE**	Mme H. Herbaux	R. Carver	J. Carver
1964	**BELLE SICAMBRE**	Mme L. Volterra	C. Bartholomew	M. Garcia
1965	**BIABEL**	G. Brun	H. Velavaud	M. Depalmas
1966	**FINE PEARL**	Baron G. de Waldner	F. Palmer	J. Massard
1967	**GAZALA**	N. B. Hunt	J. Cunnington Jr	M. Philipperon
1968	**ROSELIERE**	Mme G. Bridgland	G. Bridgland	Y. Josse
1969	**CREPELLANA**	M. Boussac	M. Vaquet	R. Poincelet
1970	**SWEET MIMOSA**	S. McGrath	S. McGrath	W. Williamson
1971	**PISTOL PACKER**	Mme A. Head	A. Head	F. Head
1972	**RESCOUSSE**	Baron de Rede	G. Watson	Y. Saint-Martin
1973	**ALLEZ FRANCE**	D. Wildenstein	A. Klimscha	Y. Saint-Martin
1974	**HIGHCLERE**	HM The Queen	W. Hern	J. Mercer
1975	NO RACE			
1976	**PAWNEESE**	D. Wildenstein	A. Penna	Y. Saint-Martin
1977	**MADELIA**	D. Wildenstein	A. Penna	Y. Saint-Martin
1978	**REINE DE SABA**	J. Wertheimer	A. Head	F. Head
1979	**DUNETTE**	Mme H. A. Love	E. Chevalier du Fau	G. Doleuze
1980	**MRS PENNY**	E. Kronfeld	I. Balding	L. Piggott
1981	**MADAM GAY**	G. Kaye	P. Kelleway	L. Piggott
1982	**HARBOUR**	Ecurie Aland	Mme C. Head	F. Head
1983	**ESCALINE**	Mme V. Fellows	J. Fellows	G. W. Moore
1984	**NORTHERN TRICK**	S. Niarchos	F. Boutin	C. Asmussen
1985	**LYPHARITA**	L. Al Swaidi	A. Fabre	L. Piggott
1986	**LACOVIA**	G. Oldham	F. Boutin	F. Head
1987	**INDIAN SKIMMER**	Sheikh Mohammed Al-Maktoum	H. Cecil	S. Cauthen
1988	**RESLESS KARA**	J. Lagardere	F. Boutin	G. Mosse
1989	**LADY IN SILVER**	M. Abdul Karim	R. Wojtowiez	A. Cruz

PRIX ROYAL-OAK

Longchamp   1m 7f

		Owner	**Trainer**	**Jockey**
1960	**PUISSANT CHEF**	H. Aubert	C. Bartholomew	M. Garcia
1961	**MATCH III**	F. Dupre	F. Mathet	F. Palmer
1962	**SICILIAN PRINCE**	G. L.-Cotton	H. Murless	L. Ward
1963	**RELKO**	F. Dupre	F. Mathet	Y. Saint-Martin
1964	**BARBIERI**	Baron G. de Rothschild	G. Watson	J. Deforge
1965	**RELIANCE**	F. Dupre	F. Mathet	Y. Saint-Martin
1966	**VASCO DA GAMA**	M. Fabiani	J. Cunnington	M. Philipperon
1967	**SAMOS III**	Countess M. Batthyany	A. Klimscha	K. Desaint
1968	**DHAUDEVI**	Mme G. Courtois	R. Corme	F. Head
1969	**LE CHOUIN**	Baron G. de Waldner	F. Palmer	A. Jezequel
1970	**SASSAFRAS**	A. Plesch	F. Mathet	Y. Saint-Martin
1971	**BOURBON**	Mme P. Wertheimer	A. Head	F. Head
1972	**PLEBEN**	Baron de Rede	G. Watson	M. Depalmas

Pat Eddery's perfectly timed run brings Dancing Brave sweeping through on the outside to win a vintage Prix de l'Arc de Triomphe in 1986. Dancing Brave now stands as a stallion at the Dalham Hall Stud in Newmarket.

1973	**LADY BERRY**	Baron G. de Rothschild	G. Watson	M. Depalmas
1974	**BUSIRIS**	N. B. Hunt	M. Zilber	F. Head
1975	**HENRI LE BALAFRE**	C. Puerari	F. Mathet	H. Samani
1976	**EXCELLER**	N. B. Hunt	F. Mathet	G. Dubroecq
1977	**REX MAGNA**	Mrs J. Couterie	F. Boutin	P. Paquet
1978	**BRAVE JOHNNY**	Miss M. Darc	C. Bartholomew	H. Samani
1979	**NINISKI**	Lady Beaverbrook	W. Hern	W. Carson
1980	**GOLD RIVER**	J. Wertheimer	A. Head	F. Head
1981	**ARDROSS**	C. A. B. St George	H. Cecil	L. Piggott
1982	**DENEL**	Mme S. Nathan	B. Secly	Y. Saint-Martin
1983	**OLD COUNTRY**	Mrs O. Abegg	L. Cumani	P. Eddery
1984	**AGENT DOUBLE**	J. Wertheimer	Mme C. Head	F. Head
1985	**MERSEY**	D. Wildenstein	P. L. Biancone	J. L. Kessas
1986	**EL CUITE**	Sheikh Mohammed Al-Maktoum	H. Cecil	S. Cauthen
1987	**ROYAL GAIT**	M. Pereira	J. Fellows	A. Gibert
1988	**STAR LIFT**	D. Wildenstein	A. Fabre	C. Asmussen
1989	**TOP SUNRISE**	C. Schmidt	A. Fabre	F. Head

PRIX DE L'ARC DE TRIOMPHE

Longchamp   1m 4f

		Owner	Trainer	Jockey
1960	**PUISSANT CHEF**	H. Aubert	C. Bartholomew	M. Garcia
1961	**MOLVEDO**	E. Verga	A. Maggi	E. Camici
1962	**SOLTIKOFF**	Mme C. del Duca	R. Pelat	M. Depalmas

1963	**EXBURY**	Baron G. de Rothschild	G. Watson	J. Deforge
1964	**PRINCE ROYAL II**	R. Ellsworth	G. Bridgland	R. Poincelet
1965	**SEA BIRD II**	J. Ternynck	E. Pollet	T. Glennon
1966	**BON MOT III**	F. Burman	W. Head	F. Head
1967	**TOPYO**	Mme L. Volterra	C. Bartholomew	W. Pyers
1968	**VAGUELY NOBLE**	Mme R. Franklin	E. Pollet	W. Williamson
1969	**LEVMOSS**	S. McGrath	S. McGrath	W. Williamson
1970	**SASSAFRAS**	A. Plesch	F. Mathet	Y. Saint-Martin
1971	**MILL REEF**	P. Mellon	I. Balding	G. Lewis
1972	**SAN SAN**	Countess M. Batthyany	A. Penna	F. Head
1973	**RHEINGOLD**	H. Zeisel	B. Hills	L. Piggott
1974	**ALLEZ FRANCE**	D. Wildenstein	A. Penna	Y. Saint-Martin
1975	**STAR APPEAL**	W. Zeitelhack	T. Grieper	G. Starkey
1976	**IVANJICA**	J. Wertheimer	A. Head	F. Head
1977	**ALLEGED**	R. Sangster	M. V. O'Brien	L. Piggott
1978	**ALLEGED**	R. Sangster	M. V. O'Brien	L. Piggott
1979	**THREE TROIKAS**	Mme A. Head	Mme C. Head	F. Head
1980	**DETROIT**	R. Sangster	O. Douieb	P. Eddery
1981	**GOLD RIVER**	J. Wertheimer	A. Head	G. W. Moore
1982	**AKIYDA**	HH Aga Khan	F. Mathet	Y. Saint-Martin
1983	**ALL ALONG**	D. Wildenstein	P. L. Biancone	W. R. Swinburn
1984	**SAGACE**	D. Wildenstein	P. L. Biancone	Y. Saint-Martin
1985	**RAINBOW QUEST**	K. Abdulla	J. Tree	P. Eddery
1986	**DANCING BRAVE**	K. Abdulla	G. Harwood	P. Eddery
1987	**TEMPOLINO**	P. de Moussac	A. Fabre	P. Eddery
1988	**TONY BIN**	Mrs V. Gaucci del Bono	L. Camici	J. Reid
1989	**CARROLL HOUSE**	A. Balzarini	M. Jarvis	M. Kinane

INDEX